THE **JAMES BACKHOUSE** LECTURES

The lectures were instituted by Australia Yearly Meeting of the Religious Society of Friends (Quakers) on its establishment in 1964.

They are named after James Backhouse who, with his companion, George Washington Walker, visited Australia from 1832 to 1838. They travelled widely, but spent most of their time in Tasmania. It was through their visit that Quaker Meetings were first established in Australia.

Coming to Australia under a concern for the conditions of convicts, the two men had access to people with authority in the young colonies, and with influence in Britain, both in Parliament and in the social reform movement. In meticulous reports and personal letters, they made practical suggestions and urged legislative action on penal reform, on the rum trade, and on land rights and the treatment of Aborigines.

James Backhouse was a general naturalist and a botanist. He made careful observations and published full accounts of what he saw, in addition to encouraging Friends in the colonies and following the deep concern that had brought him to Australia.

Australian Friends hope that this series of Lectures will bring fresh insights into the Truth, and speak to the needs and aspirations of Australian Quakerism. This particular lecture was delivered at the Australian National University, Canberra, on Monday, 5 January 2009, during the annual meeting of the Society.

Lyndsay Farrall
Presiding Clerk
Australia Yearly Meeting

2009
THE **JAMES BACKHOUSE** LECTURE

The Quaking Meeting

Transforming our selves, our meetings
and the more-than-human world

HELEN GOULD

Quakers
AUSTRALIA

ISBN 978-0-9803258-2-9

Produced by Australia Yearly Meeting of the
Religious Society of Friends (Quakers) in
Australia Incorporated

Printed by Uniprint, Hobart.

Copies may be ordered from:
Friends Book Sales, PO Box 181
Glen Osmond SA 5064 Australia.
Email: sales@quakers.org.au

About the author

Helen Gould is a seventh-generation Australian. While studying at the Australian National University she first came into contact with Quakers through the protest movement against Australia's involvement in the America-Vietnam War and the struggle for land rights for Aborigines. She began attending Canberra Meeting in 1971. In her mid-20s, she moved to Arnhem Land in the Northern Territory to teach Aboriginal children at Gotjan Jin Jirra (Cadell Outstation) where she experienced inner silence for the first time. For two years, she lived with her husband in Vanuatu among Melanesian people. They moved to Canada and attended Hamilton Meeting, then moved to Reading in the UK where Helen became a Member, and participated in a fortnightly Quaker women's group. In 1983, she and her husband returned to Australia with their two children, settling mid-way between Sydney and Newcastle. For many years, Helen regarded herself as an isolated Friend, her main involvement being through regular attendance at Yearly Meeting. During this period, she has practised hatha yoga and learned Vipassana meditation, Eastern practices she has drawn on to prepare this Backhouse Lecture. In recent years, she has been inspired by Rex Ambler's Experiment with Light to help bring Light groups to Devonshire Street, Sydney, and other Meetings in Australia. She now belongs to Wahroonga Meeting.

About the illustrator

Max Raupach has always found personal fulfilment in practising art. He has attended various workshops and read widely on Japanese and Chinese ink painting, and on the carving and printing of both woodblocks and wood engravings. After 40 years as a scientist in CSIRO doing research on soil chemistry and forestry, he finds it a great joy to use the other side of the brain as a tool to explore spiritual reality. His illustrations have been in the *Australian Friend*, *As the seed grows*, *This we can say*, and the Melbourne Summer School's *Spirit now*. He and his wife, Sonia, have been attending Adelaide Local Meeting for 23 years and have been Members for 18 years.

Synopsis

The Quaking Meeting: transforming our selves, our Meetings and the more-than-human world.

Once, Quakers quaked. Some of us still do.

I discuss individual and communal practices of Waiting Worship. My theology and practice, like that of first generation Friends, is mystical. In centring down we can directly experience God's presence: loving, divine energy sensed in our bodies, which can cause physical manifestations like quaking. Such practice transforms our lives, gradually leading us into a life of holy obedience to the Divine.

I have learned from the teachings of early Friends, both directly, and mediated through Rex Ambler's Experiment with Light. Yoga and Buddhism have also inspired me. My findings are illustrated with stories, mostly drawn from my own life, and with Max Raupach's drawings.

In Meetings for Worship we may sense a mystical communion with God through each other. This is the gift of the 'gathered meeting'.

The 'power of the Lord' made first generation Friends quake and filled them with power. We, too, can open ourselves to the loving divine energy, and to the naturally arising miracles that become possible for those who live such lives. Transformation may flow through us to others, in an ever-widening spiral, embracing the more-than-human world.

Helen Gould
21 August 2008

Contents

1. Prologue

1.1 Overview

Quakerism has been compared with a stool with three legs[1] , each necessary for its stability. To me the legs are, first, the individual's own regular spiritual practice; second, our life in Quaker community focused on Meetings for Worship, and, third, our social testimonies[2] acted out in the more-than-human world. This world includes all living beings, ecosystems, natural systems (such as the hydrological system whereby water circulates), spheres such as the biosphere, and human societies.[3] Humans are no more the *centre* of the more-than-human world than the earth is the centre of the solar system.

This lecture is my vision of what I think God calls our Australian tradition of Quakerism to be. (For a snapshot of Australian Quakers at this time, see Appendix A.) In this vision, individual mystical practice of the presence of God underpins and is in turn nourished by the group mystical practice of the Meeting for Waiting Worship, particularly when our Meetings become 'gathered'. (I'll talk about what I mean by *mystical* later in this prologue.) I discuss what helps and what hinders us in each of these practices. Then I discuss our task in the more-than-human world. In this prologue I tell you something about my spiritual journey. And in these days when some Friends[4] are likely to describe themselves as non-theist[5] or atheist, it's important to briefly explain my use of God-language.

1.2 Reading this, and writing this, as devotional practice

Patricia Loring writes:

> In the Christian tradition, devotional reading has been the foundation of all spiritual practice ... [it] is intended to feed our hearts ... to support and guide our turning to God inwardly in meditation and prayer; to help us wait on encounter, guidance, or insight should it be given us ... what makes reading devotional is a mysterious fusion in the grace of God of the content, and our intention to be opened to guidance.[6]

You may get the most benefit from this lecture if you read this as devotional practice (*lectio divina*): not to analyse it, but to *absorb* rather than *react* to it.[7] You might want to read it through once at your normal pace, to familiarise yourself with it. As you do so, be aware of any parts that particularly affect you. Then take one of those parts, and read it slowly, perhaps aloud. See if a word or phrase resonates: does it start energy (sensation or emotion) flowing in your body? If so, pay attention to that flow for as long as it lasts. You may find it helps you to retain any insights for future reflection, if you create something as a reminder.[8]

Similarly, I am practising writing this lecture mindfully, returning again and again to the Source.[9] In writing this, I am preaching what I practise.[10] Occasionally, I will use the words of others, including our ancestors in our faith, such as Isaac Penington[11], who wrote:

Be no more than God hath made thee. Give over thine own willing, give over thy own running, give over thine own desiring to know or to be anything and sink down to the seed which God sows in the heart …

However, I try to use nothing that I do not also know *experimentally*.[12] My elders in this task have listened, encouraged and challenged me.

1.3 My spiritual journey

Our practice starts with the self and from there spirals outwards. So I start by telling you something about my spiritual journey. Like most Australian Quakers I came to our practice as an adult. I was brought up rural Baptist, from which church I received two great gifts: choral hymn singing, and a thorough knowledge of the Bible. However, even at 10 years of age, I felt uneasy about the exclusivist claims of that church. How could we condemn Hindus as heathen when we knew almost nothing about them?

I am a seventh generation Australian. My ancestors were free and convict English, Irish and French. I had a difficult childhood, being moved from family to family five times in my first five years. I experienced neglect and abuse, as well as love and kindness. All children experience some kind of wounding. However loving and capable our parents are, they cannot protect us all the time. We may be powerless to meet our needs, not respected, not consistently listened to, not always protected from harm.[13] I responded to the deep pain I experienced by fleeing from my body, which feels hurts and directly knows truth, into my brain-mind, which can dissociate.

When I was 11 years old, there was a crisis in my family. I felt at that time that church elders should have known about it (if they did, they were silent) and that they should have supported me. Gradually I lost my faith in my family and in God, and when I was old enough to make my own choices, I stopped attending any church.

As a young adult, living and studying in Canberra, I was involved in the protests against the war being waged by Australia, supporting the USA, against the Vietnamese people. I also joined the struggle for land rights for Aborigines. These activities brought me into contact with Quakers and I came to Meeting. The silent Meetings eased an ache for spiritual communion, which until then I had not been aware of. I was attracted by Quakers' commitment to eradicating violence, to building peace, and by the largely silent Meetings for Worship. And I felt that I could trust these people. I kept coming to Meeting. At 21 years of age I attended a Young Friends camp and walked with them to Lake Pedder[14] before it was flooded, when it was still what Celtic Christians[15] call a 'thin' place, somewhere it is easy to feel in touch with the Spirit.

I left Canberra in my mid-20s to teach Aboriginal youngsters from a number of tribes and clans[16] living south-east from Maningrida in Arnhem Land. Among them, I had my first experience of *inner silence*. I was sitting on the back of a truck with a large group of people. The general mood was a quiet joy at driving through their country. Suddenly, I realised that I had *stopped thinking*. This was profoundly shocking, as I believed Descartes' doctrine, 'I think therefore I am', and had assumed that if I stopped thinking I would cease to exist. Now I was reflecting on an experience of existing without thought, an experience of pure presence ... could I go back there? Again, I stopped thinking, then again I reflected on it. I realised that my scepticism had been overcome because everyone else on that truck was simply being, without thinking, and that they accepted this practice as natural.

This experience changed my life; I knew the reality of the spiritual life and I knew that I must pursue it. I was already becoming aware that I was living very largely in my head and I started the long, slow and painful process of accepting all the parts of me.

I also realised the importance of having a *critical mass* of people practising, in order to break through the scepticism of many Western people.

Following my time in Arnhem Land, for two years I lived with my husband in Aoba, Vanuatu (then called the New Hebrides), among Melanesian people. Then for a year I studied anthropology in Canada, and my husband and I attended Hamilton Meeting. We moved to the UK where I joined Quakers, becoming a member of Reading Meeting. I participated in a fortnightly Quaker women's group, which I found very nourishing.[17] We returned with our children to Australia in 1983, settling mid-way between Sydney and Newcastle.

For years my main involvement with Quakers was regular attendance at Yearly Meeting. I rarely attended local Meetings because of the cost, in time and money, of getting there. However, over the last decade I have attended the two Sydney Meetings and sometimes the Hunter Valley (Newcastle) Meeting.

During the long period when I did not attend local Meetings, I sought and found spiritual nourishment elsewhere. I sang the liturgy in progressive Jewish services (my husband is Jewish). I also practised hatha yoga[18], firstly for its health benefits, later for its spiritual benefits also, and I learned Vipassana meditation[19], a Buddhist practice. I find Eastern religious practices useful because they do not have a *dualist* tradition: they do not separate and contrast mind and body, spirit and matter. I have a much more limited experience of Christian meditation.[20] Yoga and meditation have helped me to learn how to centre down and become inwardly silent. This has been extremely difficult for me, because of the alienation from my body that I mentioned earlier.

I don't find any conflict, though there is a difference in emphasis, between the Eastern practices on the one hand, and Judaism and Christianity on the other hand.[21] At the heart of Buddhism is *dhamma* (i.e. law)) and *dhamma* is good.[22] At the heart of both Judaism and Christianity, is the 'I-Thou'[23] relationship[24], of 'I' to God, and, in God, to all people, and indeed to all living beings. At its best, the quality of that relationship is love.[25]

A few years ago I discovered Rex Ambler's work.[26] Ambler re-discovered the 'method' of George Fox, which led to two books, *Light to live by* (which includes a series of guided meditations) and an anthology of Fox's writings called *Truth of the heart*.[27] David Levering and I worked together to bring Ambler's experiment with Light in the form of Light groups to Devonshire Street Meeting, Sydney, and others there joined us in leading the meditations as a collaborative effort.[28]

1.4 Mystical bodily practice

The type of Quakerism that most speaks to me is *mystical*, including when it is activist. I do not mean anything contrary to reason or scientific laws, when I use the word *mystical*. A mystical experience is simply the *direct experience*

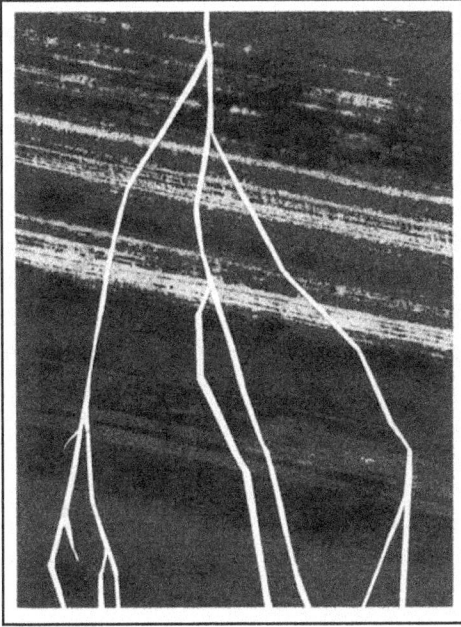

in my body, of whatever I am present to, right here and right now. Direct experience is always in the body. Whereas the mind typically fantasises about the future or reflects on the past, the body lives in the now. Here, now, the ordinary is sublime. It is possible to go deeper than words go, to experience pure presence, which some of us call God (see section 2.51). The mystic's path is a path of practising the presence of God.

Story: Dust motes and presence

One morning when I was four or five, I saw dust motes dancing in a wide shaft of sunlight. I had never noticed dust motes before, or anything seemingly unaffected by gravity, and I was entranced by their beauty.

Then I realised that I had been, for the preceding moments, fully present in that experience and completely unaware of time or indeed of anything else. 'I' as a being whose awareness was based on separateness, had briefly ceased to be. Reflecting on this at that time, I recognised that it was rare for me to be fully present, and I decided to always remember that moment of wonder.

I believe that all of us have had such experiences of presence, at least in early childhood.

I experience my body as the material expression of my spirit. So caring for my body is part of my struggle to realise our testimony to *integrity*. Whenever I have experienced psycho-spiritual healing, this has always involved a bodily change. When someone was healed in the encounter with Jesus, he often said, 'Your faith has made you whole', and he often contrasted faith with fear. Faith is akin to trust.[29] Yoga has been very fruitful. Here is an example of healing of a *relationship* which came through the body:

Story: My daughter, money and love

When my daughter was about nine years old I learned that she had been taking money from my purse and buying sweets to give to other children at school. I was distressed and at a loss as to how to deal with this behaviour. I was tentative with her because of the difficult start to our relationship. When she was ten days old we had been unavoidably separated for three weeks. I had lost the bonding I had felt with her, and I had experienced severe post-natal depression.

With my whole being I brought this new distress in prayer to the Holy One: I don't know what to do, please help us. Soon afterwards I was doing yoga asanas when suddenly a vivid image flashed into my mind. I 'saw' my baby in her little yellow knitted cap, in her Snugli carrier, snug against my breast as we ventured out for her first 'walk', before we were separated, and I felt again the unfathomable love I had felt then. I felt the heartbreak of our separation and I sobbed for a long time. Something healed in me and between us, and my daughter stopped taking money from my purse.

1.5 'God'

I don't think it really matters what words we use when talking about the ultimate reality. If 'God' gets in the way of you hearing what I am saying, please find your own translation.

Theists believe in God as creator and supreme ruler of the universe, in the words of John Shelby Spong[30], 'a being, supernatural in power, dwelling outside this world and able to invade the world in miraculous ways to bless, to punish, to accomplish the divine will, to answer prayers and to come to the aid of frail, powerless human beings'.

However, I am less interested in what people say they believe, than in what they do. A person who acts as though they are in control of their lives, for practical purposes denies the reality of God, whether they say they believe in God or not. Deborah Shaw in the *Quaker Bible Reader*[31] talks of

> resisting the pull of the culture ... Part of the culture's seduction comes in the guise of asking us to believe that there is no mystery that can't be understood or de-mystified through our intellect or effort.

I believe that we live and move and have our being within a vast mystery at the heart of all that is, and that the proper attitude to that mystery is awe. We humans will never figure it all out, for which I give thanks.

I experience, within and without me, a loving divine energy which I call God – who is not the God of the theists.

I believe in the laws of nature, and that nature is far more miraculous and mysterious than people of my culture generally know. All miracles are lawful. I believe that we, and all beings, are co-creators with the divine energy, of all that is.

I am uneasy talking 'about' God, as though God were a thing, an object among other objects. I refuse to use male pronouns for God, because of the oppression of women in so many religions. Yet, rather than saying that people's *images* of God are wrong, I would say that they are partial. As our spiritual ancestor Isaac Penington wrote[32]:

Truth is a shadow except the last, except the utmost; yet every Truth is true in its kind. It is substance in its own place, though it be but a shadow in another place (for it is but reflection from an intenser substance); and the shadow is a true shadow, as the substance is a true substance.

What is sacred is presence, flowing through all that is, from moment to moment, the 'I am' who encounters Moses.[33] I have had direct experience of this Flowing:

Story: Three days of 'enlightenment'?

Many years ago I attended a Despair and Empowerment workshop at Woodbrooke, the Quaker College in the UK.

As a child I was treated violently by an elderly male relative, and when my grandmother (also elderly) found out about it, she unwittingly compounded the damage. I felt dirty and worthless. Without being aware of it, I came to dislike and avoid elderly people. In one of the workshop exercises, I was asked to hold eye contact with a person, who happened to be old. Because I felt safe in the workshop, I had the courage to stay with the situation. Suddenly I found myself falling, falling into blackness and I was utterly terrified. Then I chose to trust that all would be well, and suddenly I found myself in a little sandy place, and a little spring of water sprang up and grew and flowed right over me and through me and washed me clean, and washed all the mud out of me so that my organs were glowing with light, and I knew, in awe, 'this is the water that Jesus gave, the living water[34], this Source is God'.

Then I became dimly aware of voices, saying: 'Is she alright? Should we call a doctor?' and I realised that I was lying on the floor. (This 'faint' may be the kind of thing that some early Friends experienced when they first heard Quaker preaching.)

For about three days I was in a state of continuous presence. I found that I was able to re-enter the experience of the well and the spring, and to explore it. First, I discovered that every human has within us an abyss and also a life-giving spring, if only we trust; then I discovered that every living being has within itself the abyss and the spring, later still I discovered that every thing that is has these within; that there is a life-giving subterranean river that flows beneath and through all that is, and that we are connected thereby with everything.

After three days it was time to return home; so I chose to return to my two-year-old daughter and my husband, knowing that with the resumption of family responsibilities, I would lose the immediacy of the experience.

Only when I read Eckhart Tolle's book *The power of now*[35] about two years ago, did I realise that I had experienced enlightenment, and that if I had only had the knowledge and appropriate support, I might have been able to remain enlightened. The enlightened person is continuously in presence. To remain so, they must live in a way that Quakers call 'holy obedience'. Thomas Kelly, a great 20th century Quaker mystic, wrote a wonderful essay on this: 'There is a degree of holy and complete obedience and of joyful self-renunciation and of sensitive listening that is breath-taking.'[36].

Endnotes

1 Marty Grundy, foreword in C. Fardelmann (ed.) *Nudged by the Spirit : stories of people responding to the still small voice of God*, Pendle Hill Publications, Wallingford, Pennsylvania, 2001, at xi-xii writes: 'The legs are the inner, personal relationship with God and the spiritual disciplines that support an interior life; corporate life in a meeting community that worships, works, hurts and heals together; and social testimonies acted out in the wider world that speak of what we are learning inwardly and together.'

2 The social testimonies include Peace-making, Simplicity, Integrity, Community and Equality. They are fruits of our practice of individual and communal worship. See *this we*

can say: Australian Quaker life, faith and thought, Australia Yearly Meeting (AYM) of The Religious Society of Friends (Quakers), 2003.

3 I learned this phrase from Susannah Brindle who found it in David Abram, *The spell of the sensuous: perceptions and language in a more-than-human world*, Pantheon Books, New York, 1996.

4 As Quakers are officially the Religious Society of Friends, we sometimes refer to ourselves as 'Friends'.

5 The leading Quaker non-theist is David Boulton (ed), *Godless for God's sake: nontheism in contemporary Quakerism*, Dales Historical Monographs, UK, 2006.

6 Patricia Loring, *Listening spirituality, Vol 1: personal spiritual practices among Friends*, Openings Press, 1997, p. 13.

7 William Taber, *Four doors to Meeting for Worship*, Pendle Hill Pamphlet (PHP) 306, 1992, p. 22, on how to listen to vocal ministry.

8 This is a kind of *lectio divina*, see Loring, p. 111.

9 'la source' in French means both source (origin) and spring of water; in pre-Christian European indigenous religions, springs were associated with female divine power.

10 Henry Cadbury 'suggested that we preach what we practise rather than practise what we preach'. See Os Cresson, 'Henry Joel Cadbury: no assurance of God or immortality' in David Boulton (ed), *Godless for God's sake*, especially pp. 94-95.

11 All but the first sentence quoted in *Quaker faith and practice: the book of Christian discipline of the Yearly Meeting of the Religious Society of Friends (Quakers) in Britain* (QFP), 1995, at 26.70.

12 As George Fox said, 'This I knew, experimentally', QFP at 19.02. Early Quakers were doing for religion what scientists of the day were doing for science: grounding their knowledge on an *experimental* method, as experienced Friends do today. Fox also contrasted 'profession', what people say they believe, with 'possession', what people know from direct experience.

13 I use the pronoun 'we' because who I am at every stage of my life is still part of who I am now. And I use it wherever I have, at one time or another, felt or acted in the way described.

14 Bob Brown, *Lake Pedder*, Wilderness Society, Hobart, 1986.

15 Celtic Christianity is incarnational and very affirming of nature; when I first discovered it, I realised it was my ancestral indigenous Christian tradition. See books by Phillip Newell and by Esther de Waal.

16 I taught at Gotjan Jin Jirra (Cadell Outstation) which was settled and visited by Burrarra, Anbarra Gunadpa, Gunguragoni, Djinang, Rembarrnga and Dangborn people. They are neighbours to the Yolngu people and have much in common with them. An excellent book, written at the request of Yolngu people, is Richard Trugden, *Why warriors*

lie down and die: towards an understanding of why the Aboriginal people of Arnhem Land face the greatest crisis in health and education since European contact: Djambatj Mala, Aboriginal Resource and Development Services Inc. Darwin, 2000, www.ards.com.au

17 I contributed to the 1984 Quaker Women's Group Swarthmore Lecture, *Bringing the invisible into the Light: some Quaker feminists speak of their experience*, Quaker Home Service, London, UK.

18 There are, traditionally, four kinds of yoga: knowledge, devotion, action and hatha. Joseph Havens has suggested adding *relationships*: see *A fifth yoga: the way of relationships*, PHP 220, 1978. Hatha yoga is the type we are most familiar with in the West; it includes asanas (postures), and much more, as steps on the way to meditation. See Swami Satyananda, *Asana pranayama mudra bandha*, 1977 & BKS Iyengar, *Light on yoga*, 1966. My teacher is Peter Mulholland of the Iyengar lineage.

19 As taught by SN Goenka. For an excellent account of Vipassana practice, see Paul Fleischman, *Cultivating inner peace: exploring the psychology, wisdom and poetry of Gandhi, Thoreau, the Buddha, and others*, 2nd edition, Pariyatti Press, Seattle. 2004, Ch. 25.

20 This tradition is largely Catholic. Christian Meditation teachers include John Main and Laurence Freeman. www.wccm.org & www.christianmeditationaustralia.org.

21 Had time permitted, I would have liked to have attempted to write this lecture in Buddhist language as well as Quaker language.

22 The laws of space-time, which include social and moral law, are, I believe, based on love. See George Ellis, *Faith, hope and doubt in times of uncertainty: combining the realms of scientific and spiritual inquiry*, 2008 Backhouse Lecture, The Religious Society of Friends (Quakers) in Australia.

23 Martin Buber, *I and Thou*, Charles Scribner's Sons, New York, c. 1970.

24 Ironically, the way we talk about relationships in English is impoverished in comparison with Australian Aboriginal languages (which are being extinguished by English). Non violent communication is also much more sensitive to the *relationship* implications of language than English. See Marshall Rosenberg, *Non violent communication: a language of life*, Centre for Non Violent Communication, USA, 2003.

25 I sense that Buddhism on the one hand, and Judaism and Christianity on the other, are less different than they appear. Buddhism affirms the 'Thou'-ness of all living beings. However, there is, in prophetic Judaism and Christianity, an emphasis on resistance to harmful social structures and institutions that is absent from Buddhism.

26 Ambler's Experiment with Light does not depend on 'God' language, making it accessible to non-theists and to atheists.

27 Rex Ambler, *Light to live by: an exploration in Quaker spirituality*, Quaker Books, London, 2002. Also *Truth of the heart: an anthology of George Fox*, 2001, same publisher.

28 I have also led a once-weekly, six-week Light Group 'course' at Wahroonga Meeting, and weekend workshops for Canberra Meeting at Helen Bayes' property at Cherrybush.

29 John MacMurray is useful: *Ye are my Friends* and *To save from fear*, Quaker Home Service, London, 1979.

30 John Shelby Spong, *Jesus for the non-religious: recovering the Divine at the heart of the human*, Harper Collins, 2007, p. 222.

31 Deborah Shaw in Paul Buckley & Stephen Angell (eds), *The Quaker Bible reader*, Earlham School of Religion, 2006.

32 QFP at 27.22

33 My song 'Bushwalk' is based on that insight. See *This we can say* 1.51.

34 The wonderful story of Jesus and the Samaritan woman at Jacob's well is told in John 4:14. Jesus said, 'Anyone who drinks the water that I shall give will never be thirsty again: the water that I shall give will turn into a spring inside him, welling up to eternal life' (Jerusalem Bible).

35 Eckhart Tolle, *The power of now: a guide to spiritual enlightenment*, Hodder Australia, 2004.

36 These experiences are understood and supported in many Buddhist circles. For example, a Zen master who is enlightened, and who senses that a student is close to enlightenment, will sometimes propel him or her into that state, through using his or her gaze. George Fox also used his gaze to grow people spiritually; there are several examples in his Journal.

2. Individual practice of waiting worship

In this section I present the method that I use for practising waiting worship on my own. This practice is based on early Friends' practice[1], and is enriched by insights from yoga and my experience with the Experiment with Light. I write about waiting worship because early Friends were more likely to use a phrase such as 'waiting upon the Lord' than 'worship'. Think of the idea of a lady in waiting – she does not know whether or when she will be summoned to serve, and her task is to be in constant readiness with an attitude of humility and thankfulness, whether she is called to serve or not.

2.1 A very brief survey of spiritual practices

Spiritual teachers everywhere teach that progress on the path requires regular practice. The paradoxical goal[2] of all practices is what the Buddhists call mindfulness, and what Brother Lawrence calls 'the practice of the presence of God'[3]: one meaning is to practise consciously letting go of whatever interferes with direct awareness of what is present, here and now.

Jesus' spiritual practices included prayer, fasting, celebration, retreat, time alone with God in nature, scripture reading, participating in the religious life of his worshipping community, and loving engagement with others including children.[4] Early Friends' spiritual practices included all of Jesus' practices, and also writing spiritual autobiographies, better known as journals.

In my own life I have found it impossible to sustain my practice without making it very high priority. I had to simplify my life: taking work that did not demand too much energy, reducing my circle of friends and acquaintances, and being very selective about cultural events I attended. What is possible depends, of course, on one's life stage and responsibilities. I am fortunate to have retired. Creative activities like painting, dancing, music-making and journalling can help. Surfing, bushwalking, skiing or sailing can also be opportunities for practising presence.[5] One Friend gets up early and returns again and again to mindfulness while showering, dressing and eating. Any activity which helps us to be present in the moment connects us to God.

2.2 The practice

First, I prepare my body to be fully attentive, so mainly I do it early in the morning while I am fresh and before eating. I often start with a walk or with yoga. Then I sit in a position which grounds me, which I know I can sustain for a long time, and where my spine is free to stretch.

I acknowledge God's presence, in gratitude, for the Holy One is always here. William Taber[6], speaking of individual and communal worship, wrote:

> I once thought worship was something I *do*, but for many years now it has seemed as if worship is actually a state of consciousness which I *enter*, so that I am immersed into a living, invisible stream of reality which has always been present throughout all history. In some mysterious way this stream unites me with the communion of the saints across the ages, and brings me into the presence of the Living Christ.

By entering the stream we both nourish ourselves, and replenish the stream itself.

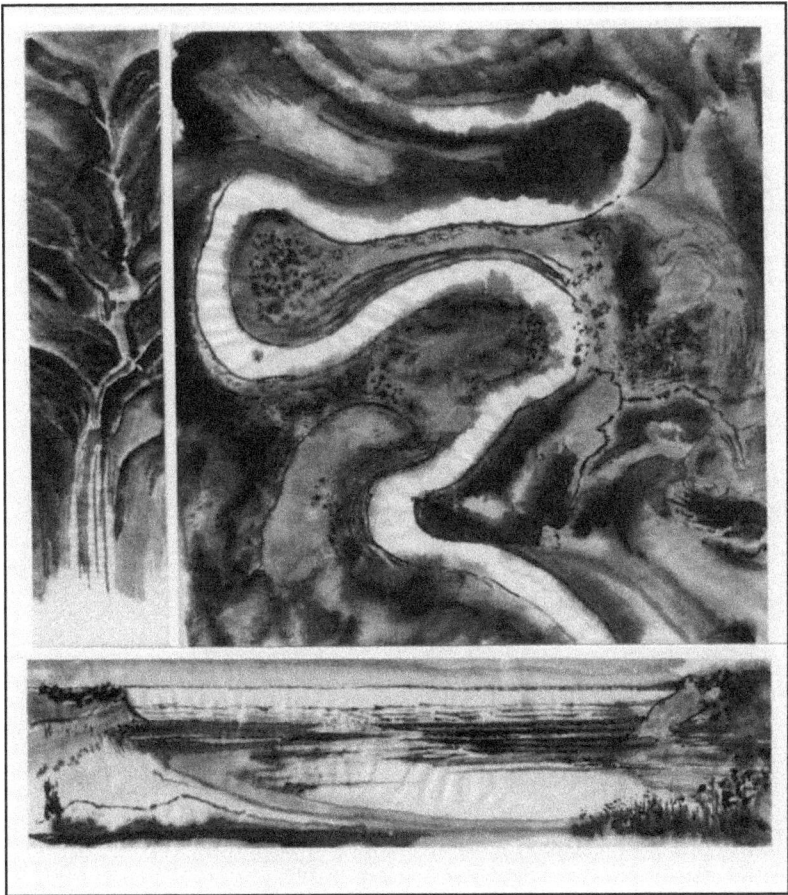

So here is my version of the practice. I am hoping that some of you might try it for yourselves, so I am writing it as a series of suggestions.

Become still.

Bring your awareness to your centre, just below your belly button. Notice what wants your awareness there.

Let yourself become silent.

> - As thoughts arise, notice them and welcome them.
>
> - As images arise, notice them and welcome them.
>
> - As emotions arise, notice them and welcome them.
>
> - As sensations arise, notice them and welcome them.

Whatever arises, it will change[7].

Or simply observe the breath.

Gradually, you will begin to experience moments of emptiness.

This is how you make space – so that you can listen.

The Holy Presence usually speaks very softly.

Presence comes with a change in the body sensations – a felt shift.[8]

Sometimes thoughts and images arise that show you that you have been out of the Light[9],

-   doing something that is not right for you to do

-   or failing to do something that is right for you to do.

Again, this awareness comes with bodily sensation. Offer this situation to God: 'This is my reality right now. Help me!' And let it go.

Return to the practice of expectant waiting, of emptying.

Prayers of petition may arise:

> 'May I grow more loving towards this person.'
>
> 'May I release my bitterness about this situation.'
>
> 'May this person receive an opportunity to ease his anxiety.'

As prayers arise, inwardly pray them and release them.

If a felt shift comes with a message that there is something specific to do, then do it. If you feel blocked, pray for guidance.

And gradually, or sometimes blindingly, more light will be given.[10]

In summary

Centre

Be still

Trust

Breathe

Notice

Welcome

Thank

You may experience, in your heart or belly, a sensation and attitude of gratitude and praise.

2.3 Notes to help with the practice

2.3.1 Becoming still and centring down[11]

In English we commonly refer to four main directions: north, south, east and west. Many other peoples include as directions, up and down. Of course, God is in every direction. However, deeply implicit in much Jewish and Christian thought is the view that God is 'up' there: this usage goes back to early images of God as a sky deity. If, when you worship, you raise your eyes upwards, 'towards the heavens', your chin will tend to go up. You are likely to be thinking a lot, and you will tend to think about the future.[12]

Here are some hints to reduce active thinking: rest the tongue lightly on the palate behind the top teeth and keep it still. Also keep the eyes still and lightly closed or semi-focused, pointing slightly downward and inward. Emphasise the out-breath a little more than the in-breath.

On the other hand, if your chin falls forward, you may get sleepy and you will tend to dwell on the past. Emphasise the in-breath, and bring your chin up. There is a beautiful point of balance of the head, where the mind can become still, and present. If you get sleepy, open your eyes, keeping the gaze soft.

Friends talk of coming to Meeting for Worship, sitting and centring *down*: down from the brain towards the heart or lower.[13] We can centre down by paying attention to the centre of our bodies. To find your centre, practise standing or sitting in stillness, and sense for that in you which is midway between left and right side, between up and down. Let yourself become balanced and grounded. Return again and again to this space when you lose concentration. It is also very important that the spine be free to move and that you not slump. Allow your belly to come back into your back.

The final two directions I want to draw your attention to are *inward* and *outward*. We Quakers often speak of experiencing or listening deeply and we are referring here to the inwardness of centring.

In sacred geometry God is viewed as a circle.[14] It has been said that God is a circle whose circumference is nowhere, and whose centre is everywhere.[15] God is the Beyond that is Within.[16] Six-year-old Anna in that great mystical work *Mister God, this is Anna*[17] understood this well:

'Where are you?" [Anna] had said.
'Here, of course,' I [Finn] replied.
'Where's me, then?'
'There!'
'Where do you know about me?'
'Inside myself someplace.'
'Then you know my middle in your middle.'
'Yes, I suppose so.'
'Then you know Mister God in my middle in your middle, and everything you know, every person you know, you know in your middle. Every person and everything that you know has got Mister God in their middle and so you have got their Mister God in your middle too – It's easy.'

The deeper inward we are able to go, the more power-filled is our return outward.

2.3.2 The breath

The Hebrew word *ruach* which is usually translated as *spirit* also means breath and wind. Try thinking of our breath as God's Spirit breathing through us. In the words of early Friend Isaac Penington:

> God is near to every man with the breath of his life, breathing upon him at times according to his pleasure; which, man's spirit opening unto, and drinking in, it becometh a seed or principle of life in him, overspreading and leavening him up to eternal life.[18]

We inspire – breathe in; and expire – breathe out.[19] Breathing is unique among bodily processes in that all of us are familiar with controlling it voluntarily (e.g. suppressing a sneeze) and yet mostly we breathe without any awareness. So the breath is a link between the aware mind and our unconscious. Observing it teaches us much about who we really are.

One way to foster stillness through paying attention to the breath is to observe the breath at the entrance to the nostrils and above the upper lip. Practise following the breath from the beginning of the inhalation, to the pause, exhalation, pause … notice changes in sensation from in-breath to out-breath. As you become aware of having lost concentration, gently return to the practice.[20]

When you are skilled at becoming still and letting the thoughts go, simply observe your breath at your centre. Pay attention to the sensations accompanying the rise and fall of the diaphragm that separates your chest from your abdomen. I find it important, at first, to breathe completely, down to the base of the belly and all the way up to swell the collarbones. In my experience, when my belly is loose and the breathing is concentrated there, I am likely to have negative thoughts and feelings of depression, concentrating on myself (e-motioning inwards). Whereas when I am praying for others, and feeling compassion (e-motioning outwards), I am breathing the full breath. However, as I go deeper within, my breath will change. It may become very light.

The only time when it is possible for us to be completely still is at the turning of the breath: between the in- and out-breath and between the out- and in-breath. I pay particular attention to this moment of stillness; this is the moment when I am more likely to receive insight.

Our Friend Isaac Penington understood these practices well:

> By the stirring of life in the soul, desires after life are kindled ... the spring stirring, the soul cannot but move towards its centre ... That man who is born of the Spirit is to wait for the movings, breathings, and kindlings of the Spirit in him." [21]

2.3.3 The heart, the belly, the womb

When you have centred down, bring your awareness to your heart and feel it. Feel how open it is, how tender it is. Feel without judging, just observing. And if you do judge yourself, just observe that. When we just observe, there is an opportunity for the Light to show us what is really going on in our lives. To open the heart is to trust. The heart is the place where forgiveness happens. We do the work, prepare ourselves, and it comes upon us as grace. The heart is where gratitude is felt as sensations of openness, ease and thankfulness radiating outwards. [23]

Heart, as used in the Bible and by early Friends, may mean far more than typically it does for us today. The Hebrew word *rechem* which is usually translated in English versions of the Bible as *heart*, also means belly, womb, inward parts and bowels. The related verb *rachem* means to have pity on, to feel compassion, to be merciful. [22]

2.3.4 Body prayer: walking, sitting and more

Our bodies are temples of the living God. Paying attention to what feels *alive* in my body helps me to grow into God-centeredness. One can also use posture as a body prayer. Religious practices may include dance, or kneeling, standing, bowing, hand positions and the like to prepare one to experience the living presence. When I am struggling with issues of humbly letting go of self and yielding to God's will, I use the Moslem prayer posture of submission.

Early Friends walked a great deal. Walking rhythm relates to rhythms of breath and heartbeat. Walking outdoors with a silent mind, simply being present with the more-than-human world or concentrating on every body movement, is a very powerful practice.[23] There is wisdom in the ancient Jewish law limiting the distance one can walk on the Sabbath so that people were obliged to live within walking distance of the synagogue. Try walking mindfully the last few blocks to Meeting. This will help you to centre down.

Mostly we sit down to worship. To centre down takes both relaxation and alertness. It's hard to sit for long unless your abdominal muscles and lower back are strong. Sitting, especially on the floor and especially at ground level, reminds our bodies that the earth always supports us, and that God is down as well as up. When I sit in a chair to worship, I sit slightly forwards, my feet on the floor, with my chest open and my spine free to stretch. I let my head find that point of balance. My palms face upwards, wrists soft and relaxed. Ruth Tod, a Quaker who is training to teach the Alexander technique[24], wrote:

> [I allow] my belly to come back into my back so that I am centred. Instead of lurching forward into action, I allow a pool of calm to emerge in front of me. I become both more present in myself and more open to receive.

2.3.5 Quaking

I sometimes vibrate or quake when I am practising individual or group worship. It only comes when I am becoming very centred. Sometimes as I have some insight a release of energy causes me to gently shake, or I may feel a shudder up my spine. In yoga this is called *kundalini* energy.[25]

Deborah Shaw[26] described other physical manifestations of Spirit, including weeping, and tingles or goose flesh, which I also sometimes experience in individual and group worship:

With me it happens when I am in a spiritual conversation with someone and either one of us is given a capital 'T' truth to share, I will recognise it through the experience of the hair on my head standing on end ... John Calvi[27] shared that the body both beckons and receives the Spirit ... there are ways that compassion and wisdom flow between us that we have only the barest understanding of and ... *fear interrupts that flow* and interrupts the quaking ... [my emphasis].

When something I am reading speaks to me, I feel a cool breeze flowing in my lower arms and legs up into my body. When I hear something that 'moves' me, I feel the energy rising in my body.

2.4 Helps and hindrances

I have experienced a number of helps and hindrances to doing and establishing this practice; what follows is far from comprehensive.[28]

- **Spiritual companions.** I am eternally grateful for my elders and others with whom I can talk about these matters and, on occasion, with whom I can worship.

- **Wider culture.** An uncomprehending and occasionally hostile wider culture is a significant hindrance.[29] It can be difficult to regularly set aside time and you may feel awkward in prioritising this and explaining to others. I certainly felt not entitled to take this time 'for myself' and it took me a long time before I actually gave my worship time the priority I accorded it in my heart.

- **Noise and vibrations.** As mentioned above, one way I experience 'the power of the Lord' is as vibrations in my body. Of course, I can train myself to centre down despite the background hum of air-conditioning, fluorescent light, electric clock or refrigerator, not to mention telephones. But all these little assaults on the silence add up, so that it takes longer to centre down. Outer and inner noises are less in the early morning and my mind is fresher, so I find it a good time for practice.

- **Valuing *being* as well as *doing*.** Most Friends I know live very hectic lives. We get overstimulated with too many people and experiences for us to reflect on and integrate into our lives. I often have an active mind and find that it takes considerable time for the inner noise to subside. However, our worth does not depend on *doing*; we are true children of God, just by *being*.[30]

Among the Aboriginal people whom I knew in central Arnhem Land, everyone was able to sing and to paint. The boys would pass around a length of pipe to practise playing didgeridoo and there was no sense that it mattered how 'good' you were; for the first time I felt valued just because I was, not because I was 'good' at doing certain things. I found this profoundly moving.

I was also moved to learn that in the Wiradjuri language of south-western NSW, 'good' is the primary reality, and the word for 'evil' is simply 'non-good'. From these two very different Aboriginal peoples we can learn what the Bible affirms – that what God created was 'very good'[31], and that includes us.

-    **Perseverance**. If we are 'hooked' on busyness, then our withdrawal symptoms will include boredom. By making a firm determination to stay with the practice despite the boredom, I have learned much about myself. Silence and stillness are the absence of fear. It may be emotionally painful – just observe and learn.[32]

-    **Time**. Practice needs to be regular, and it needs to be long enough for the worshipper to settle, especially when one is dealing with noise and inner agitation.

-    **Relationship with food**. Fox spoke in his journal about an occasion when large numbers of people came to hear him preach. He discerned that they needed to be 'famished from speaking' so he waited a long, long time for them to become silent before he spoke. This is a form of fasting which certainly helps practice.

When I am too busy I lose my centredness in God and I over-eat to fill that hunger. Lacking God's gift of manna[33] for this moment, of energy for right now, I may crave a sugar hit. Other people may lose their connections with their bodies' needs and neglect to eat enough. For me the challenge is to listen, and observe what is getting in the way of my paying attention.

Moreover, the wrong foods, or too much or too little food, or a very recent meal, may interfere with spiritual practice.

- **Comfort**. Physical comfort helps, whereas stiffness, pain or tiredness may hinder practice. Regular exercise and adequate rest often helps. However, some people live with chronic and intractable pain. Some of the saints suffered chronic illnesses, yet they were able to use their physical condition to yield up control of their lives to the Divine.[34] Taber wrote that 'moments of pain or frustration can be converted into brief times of secret prayer for ourselves and blessing for the problem.' [35]

- **Confidence in one's ability**. As Taber observed, we have a 'rich, inborn capacity to be alive to the spiritual dimension'. I learned by just doing it, by practising the Experiment with Light, and by talking to experienced, contemplative Friends. Also it's important not to overlook the little insights, for mostly this is what the Light shows us; in responding faithfully to them, our capacity for listening to the Light will grow.[36]

- **Immersion in nature**. Immersion in nature is vital for many of us. Jesus and also early Friends had far more contact with the natural world than most of us. Jesus and Fox were very familiar with sowing and reaping. Both knew how to care for sheep. Both rejoiced in the birds.[37] Such experiences nourish the soul, providing rich sources of imagery. Spring, summer and autumn have more meaning because of a winter keenly felt. Part of the challenge facing white Australians in becoming native is to attune ourselves to the rhythms of nature in this holy land where we actually live.

Aboriginal spirituality can help us. Miriam Rose Ungunmerr-Baumann of the Daly River people wrote:

> the greatest gift (our people) can share is called *dadirri*. It is inner, deep listening and quiet, still awareness. *Dadirri* recognises the deep spring that is inside us. We call on it and it calls to us. This is the gift that the world is thirsting for. When I experience *dadirri*, I am made whole again. I can sit on the river bank

or walk through the trees; even if someone close to me has passed away, I can find my peace in this silent awareness. There is no need of words. A big part of *dadirri* is listening …" [38]

2.5 Embodied practice and early Friends

Early Friends had an easier time than we do in learning this practice. Quaker preachers taught it, the mainstream culture supported spiritual questing, and early Friends had fewer distractions than we do. There was far less noise and vibration, they didn't seek entertainments and the circle of people they met was usually far smaller. Early Friends were far more in contact with their bodies than we usually are. They did far more physical work, and mostly they walked or rode a horse from place to place. They were far more likely to witness sickness and death, and birth. They had more skills with their hands than we have. It appears that they learned to centre down easily[39], and they were often able and willing to devote more time to individual and group worship than we are.

2.5.1 The 'power of the Lord'

The phrase 'the power of the Lord' and its variants occurs 388 times in Fox's writing, more than twice as often as variants of the much better known phrase 'that of God in everyone'.[40] The widely held view is that Friends used it to refer to a power that they felt within, and attributed to God, and that this power enabled them to meet situations of peril and persecution with courage, often transforming the situation and their persecutors as well.

However 'the power of the Lord' means more than this. Early Friends used the phrase to refer to divine energy sensed in their bodies, assuring Friends of their unity with divine purpose.[41] Experiences of 'the power' include quaking and similar energy flows as described above. Scott Martin has likened George Fox to a Qi Gong[42] master and healer.[43] In a gathered Meeting for Worship at Yearly Meeting, I have experienced divine energy flowing through my body, healing me physically and spiritually.[44]

When you are in a state of presence, you will feel the body sensations change – a felt shift – and this is an experience of energy moving through your body, perhaps making you vibrate (or 'quake'), laugh, cough, yawn, blush, or something else. The yogis say that this energy movement clears the *chakras*.[45] The yogic practices of *pranayama* (breath energy work) and *bandhas* (body locks) teach one how to observe and augment the energy flows. This is a great help to becoming aware of the spontaneous movements of the Spirit within us.[46]

As we attend to our centre and become aware of these movements of Spirit, we receive power to do God's will in the world. Isaac Penington[47] expressed this eloquently:

> There is a pure seed of life which God hath sown in thee; Oh, that it might come through, and come over all that is above it, and contrary to it. And for that end, wait daily to feel it, and to feel thy mind subdued by it, and joined to it. Take heed of looking out in the reasonings of thy mind, but dwell in the feeling sense of life, and then, that will arise in thee more and more, which maketh truly wise, and gives power, and brings into the holy authority and dominion of life.

For the very first generation of Friends, the public meetings included spectacular physical manifestations of Spirit.[48] These were the 'threshing' meetings, where people quaked in a way that evoked the image of seed being winnowed to rid it of the chaff. Tarter wrote[49]:

> The act of quaking was an act laden with meaning and purpose: it was the motion of spiritual rebirth and apocalyptic delivery, both literally and metaphorically, in and through the sacralized body.

And again:

> Charles Marshall graphically recounted the corporeal manifestations of spirit at meetings he attended ... 'But ah! The seizings of soul, and prickings at heart,

which attended that season! Some fell on the ground, others cried out under the sense of their states …' In another missive, he described his prophetic motion in terms of physical labour, being 'made to cry like a woman in travail'.[50]

Outside the context of Meeting for Worship, I have experienced something similar. I had the privilege of living among Aboriginal people, and later among Vanuatan people. In both communities, while I was there, a child died, and I experienced the deep, gut-wrenching wailing of their mothers and sisters. Later, when I felt a deep grief that sat like a lead weight at the base of my belly, I chose to take time apart, remove all distractions, and simply open my mouth and let my breath do what it would, and a deep wail broke out until I had no more breath, and I wailed again and again, until I was cleansed and healed.

2.6 The Experiment with Light [51]

The Experiment with Light[52], originally developed by Rex Ambler, is a powerful guided practice distilled from writings of early Friends, which is very similar to the practice given above.[53] It is usually easier to learn in a Light group than to learn on your own.

In their individual worship and in the 'settled' meetings[54], early Friends sat for however long it took in order to let their minds settle and become empty and receptive. They didn't consciously seek to explore sources of uneasiness in their lives, as is done in the Experiment with Light; rather, as you become 'still and cool in your own mind from your own thoughts' [55], you will become aware of anything that gets in the way of that inner stillness. I have over time uncovered layer upon layer of 'impurities', subtle ways in which I am out of the presence, separating myself from God. I resonate with Isaac Penington's advice:

Wait to feel the light of life [uncovering what is amiss] and drawing [thee] from the evil; and let it choose what it shall please first to discover and draw [thee] from. And though it be little and very inconsiderable in thine eyes, yet dispute not – but where the light first begins to lead, do thou there begin to follow.[56]

28

Ambler's method can be expressed in the acronym MOWS: Mind the light, Open your heart to the truth, Wait in the light, and Submit to the truth. Before we start, I lead the group in gentle stretching and then a body awareness exercise, in order to help us to centre and become still and silent. Our teaching is not about issues of theology or society. It is about how to listen to the Light within, for that inner guide will teach each one what we need to do in our own particular conditions. What the Light shows is unique to each individual, for each is at a different stage on our spiritual journey. Our practice is experimental.

Ambler describes how Fox 'turned the people from the darkness to the light'. People were to look for

> signs of disturbance in themselves: twitches of conscience, feelings of oppression, anxiety … They were then to look at the situation that those feelings referred to, and to let the reality of it be opened to them. They had to be still and silent for this to happen, to adopt an attitude of openness and expectancy, otherwise their own thoughts and fears would take over. If they were open, however, they would begin to see things they had never seen before. The spirit deep within them would shed light on what was going on in their life, what they were doing or not doing, and why. It would show them the truth about themselves. If they accepted the truth revealed, however difficult, they would see everything else more clearly, not least how they could now live their lives more freely and fully.

In developing the Experiment with Light, Ambler also drew on Eugene Gendlin's method called Focusing.[57] This method was itself partly informed by Quakerism.[58] The method is taught methodically, in small steps, and learners are listened into the practice by a teacher or focusing partner. It is a more embodied practice than the meditations taught by Ambler. Gendlin said:

> Every bad feeling is potential energy towards a more right way of being if you give it space to move towards its rightness … The very existence of bad feelings

within you is evidence that your body knows what is wrong and what is right. It must know what it would be like to feel perfect, or it could not evoke a sense of wrong.[59]

I use a Focusing version of the guided practice, when I lead Light groups.

In the next section, I will briefly compare and contrast Light groups with Meetings for Worship.

2.7 Towards holy obedience: fruits of the practice

Our individual and communal practices of waiting worship grow the loving kindness in us, and love's companion, humility. The early Quakers emphasised this. Barclay said that our teaching concerning how to worship God is that all must 'lay aside their own will-Worship and voluntary acts performed in their own wills ...'[60] This self-sacrifice is the core message of William Penn's 'No Cross, no Crown'[61], and it is a frequent theme of Isaac Penington[62] and also George Fox.[63] It is, to Quakers, the key message of the crucifixion: that if we humbly do what the Spirit requires of us, then, yes, we shall go through darkness and suffering, we shall lose our selves, we may, like Jesus, feel abandoned by God, and we shall be brought through this to a new resurrected self, centred in the divine. The paradox is that by giving up our selves we become more truly our selves.

As Fox says, this process will show me my wrong-doing. Margaret Fell wrote:

> let the eternal light search you ... it will rip you up and lay you open ... naked and bare before ... God from whom you cannot hide yourselves ... Therefore give over deceiving of your souls." [64]

And when I do see my wrong-doing, what am I to do? I have learned through experience that the only way is to humble myself. I must open myself to feel the situation thoroughly in all its aspects, accept full responsibility, and mourn. Moreover, it is only when I mourn that repentance is real, so that

I am no longer at risk of repeating the behaviour. As I do so, clarity comes. I discern the next step (which may involve making amends), I ask for help to change my ways of behaving, and then act on any directions I receive. Then I must bring it back into worship, for reflection, and finally I simply let it go.[65] In my experience, the process really hurts, yet in the end I feel gratitude, joy, and ease in my heart.

I am very grateful for a related learning, which is that my responsibility is to make amends to the other person for my own wrong-doing and not worry about any ways in which that person may have upset or harmed me. If I am in wrong relationship with them, they are not going to hear what I might want to say about their behaviour. If I make amends unconditionally, space may open in them for them to hear the Inner Teacher on these matters.

Jesus said, 'You shall love the Lord your God... and the second commandment is like unto it, You shall love your neighbour as yourself.'[66] You cannot truly love God or others unless you love yourself, and vice versa. Jesus also taught that we are to love our enemies, and I think that this includes the parts of ourselves that we do not like and are, perhaps, ashamed of. By paying loving attention to those parts, holding them in the light of presence, we will discover more about the needs of these parts, and we give them an opportunity to change and heal.[67]

Humility means closeness to the earth, accepting our limitations as humans. Being grounded, the humble person is not concerned about whether she is poorly regarded – or showered with honours. It is all one to her. She feels neither inferior to nor superior to any other being. Such distinctions make no sense. She simply rejoices in being a living being connecting with other living beings, and able to use her gifts in God's way.

There is a wonderful Hasidic[68] teaching:

Keep two truths in your pocket, and take them out according to the need of the moment. Let one be: 'For my sake was the world created.' And the other: 'I am but dust and ashes.'

Over time, even when you are active in the world, you will intermittently become aware of the sensations in your centre, guiding you. Now worship is becoming habitual and constant. To the extent that one is living from one's centre, constantly attending and submitting to what presence requires, one is living a life of holy obedience.

There is a beautiful illustration of obedience to guidance from the life of our Friend Margaret Wilkinson[69]. Margaret used her growing blindness as an opportunity to hone her skills of listening and responding to inner guidance.

In 1967 southern Tasmania was ravaged by bushfires; many people lost their lives, and many more lost their homes. Margaret helped to counsel those who had lost family or homes in the fires. One day she received inner guidance that she must visit one of the women she had counselled. This was not easy, it was pouring with rain and she had to organise someone to drive her the long distance involved. But she went. Eventually she arrived at the woman's caravan. She knocked at the door but there was no answer. Again she knocked and called out, there was no response. She tried again. After fifteen minutes she turned and went away. Months or years later, she met the caravan-dweller, who said to her, 'Do you recall when you came to my caravan and knocked and called out and there was no answer?' 'Yes,' replied Margaret. 'Well, I was there. I had a bottle of pills in my hand [to take her life] and when you knocked I did not have the strength to respond. But I knew that you cared about me.'

Endnotes

1 See Rex Ambler, *Truth of the heart* ss. 1:1, 31, 34, 40, 41, 61, 69, 89, 91; 2:1, 18, 79, 81; Isaac Penington, *The light within & selected writings*; Keiser and Moore *Knowing the mystery of life within*; Elizabeth Gray Vining, *William Penn: mystic as reflected in his writings* PHP 167; Sterling Olmsted, *Motions of love: Woolman as mystic and activist*, PHP 312.

2 The 'goal' is paradoxical because ultimately one must let go of it in order to experience it.

3 . Brother Lawrence of the Resurrection, *The practice of the presence of God*, Spire Books, Old Tappan, N.J., c.1958.

4 See Joseph Havens, *A fifth yoga: the way of relationships*, PHP 220, 1978.

5 Gary Bouma, *Australian soul: religion and spirituality in the 21st century*, Cambridge University Press, 2006.

6 W Taber, *Four doors to Meeting for Worship*, PHP 306, p. 6.

7 You can simplify the practice by simply paying attention to *sensations*, letting all else (thoughts, emotions, images, etc.) go. This is one kind of Buddhist Vipassana practice. Often, my experience is of my mind slowing down and my entering a sort of reverie in which I may experience an extended stream of thought, or of images, only after quite some time becoming aware of this and patiently returning to the practice. However, the extended flow is often very helpful.

8 'felt shift' is Gendlin's term for the change in body sensations. See Eugene Gendlin, *Focusing: how to gain direct access to your body's knowledge*, 2nd edn, Rider, Random House, London, 2003.

9 Some people actually experience a light, many do not. The experience can be literal or metaphorical. Either way is fine. The common experience of the Light showing us that something is not right in our lives is dealt with well in Ambler, *Light to live by*, Quaker Books, London and also by Taber at pp. 19-20.

10 Caroline Fox QFP 26.04. Caroline Fox (1819-1871) wrote in her journal: 'The first gleam of light, the first cold light of morning, which gave promise on day with its noontide glories, dawned on me one day at meeting, when I had been meditating on my state in great depression. I seemed to hear the words articulated in my spirit, "Live up to the light thou hast, and more will be granted thee." Then I believed that God speaks to man by His Spirit …' This has been reworked as a beautiful song by Canadian Friend Susan Stark, 'Live up to the Light'.

11 See Diana Lampen, 'Practical issues', in J Lampen (ed), *Seeing, hearing, knowing: reflections on Experiment with Light*, William Sessions Ltd, York, England, 2008. .

12 Perhaps the 'up'ness of God in Judeo-Christian theology has contributed to the Christian emphasis on the end-time, and life after death, to the tragic neglect of here and now.

13 The centre is known in yoga as the *manipura chakra* (ego issues), in Japanese Zen as the *hara*, in Taoism as the *dan tien*, and is also recognised by the Ngarrindjerri people of South Australia and probably other Aboriginal peoples.

14 Miranda Lundy, *Sacred Geometry*, Wooden Books, UK, 1998.

15 Attributed to many sources including Nicholas de Lille and Pascal.

16 Coined by Emil Boutroux, one of the terms that Rufus Jones used for God; see Vining: *Friend of life: the biography of Rufus Jones*, Lippincott, Philadelphia 1958, p. 258.

17 Fynn, *Mister God, this is Anna*, HarperCollins Religious, 1974, pp. 80-81.

18 *Some questions and answers showing man his duty* (1662) in Keiser & Moore, 276. *The New Covenant of the Gospel distinguished from the Old Covenant of the Law* (1660) II.74-75 (reprinted Keiser & Moore 152).

19 In yoga there is a body of teaching called *pranayama*: exercises for regulating the energy through altering breathing. See Satyananda, *Asana pranayama mudra bandha*, or BKS Iyengar, *Light on yoga*, Allen & Unwin, UK, 1966.

20 The upper lip is the governing meridian in Chinese energy work; sensations in any part of the body will affect the sensations here, which makes this area a very powerful place to get in touch with one's being as a whole.

21 *The New Covenant of the Gospel distinguished from the Old Covenant of the Law* (1660) Works II, 74-75, reprinter Keiser & Moore, p. 152.

22 Michele Lise Tarter, 'Quaking in the Light: the politics of Quaker women's corporeal prophecy in the seventeenth-century Transatlantic World', in *A Centre of wonders: the body in Early America*, ed. Janet Moore Lindman & Michele Lise Tarter. Cornell University Press, Ithaca, 2001, pp. 145-162. Tarter at p. 149 writes: 'Seeking to know and feel God through rachem — in Hebrew etymology, the word for the bowels, the womb, as well as compassion and mercy — men and women Friends surrendered to the experience of the divine feminine as it rose and fell in their bodies.'

23 Thich Nhat Hanh, *Walking meditation*, Eastern Press, New Haven, USA, 1985. See also, the Buddha's *Sattipathana sutta*. In Christianity the practice of walking a labyrinth is similar.

24 See Ruth Tod's article in *The Friend*, 7 March 2008, pp. 10-11.

25 See Marcelle Martin 'Giving birth to the Sun' in M Gilpin (ed), *Discovering God as companion*, Author House, Bloomington, USA, 2007, pp. 19-24.

26 Deborah Shaw, 'Being fully present to God', Michener Lecture 2005, Southeastern Yearly Meeting of the Religious Society of Friends, USA, pp. 33-34.

27 John Calvi is a well-known Quaker healer who has written a PHP and an article in Charlotte Fardelmann, *Nudged by the Spirit*, Pendle Hill Publications, Wallingford, USA, 2001.

28 Eastern religions recognise a number of hindrances to meditation. See, for example, the Buddha's *Satipatthana sutta*. I have not drawn explicitly from these, preferring to use my own experience and insights.

29 See David Tacey, *Re-enchantment : the new Australian spirituality*, HarperCollins, 2000.

30 Marlou Carlson writes movingly about the connection between her busyness and her belief that her worth depended on her *doing* worthwhile things, rather than just on *being*: 'If I was not doing good works, I was nobody. For years I had been committing the great sin of not believing I was a worthy soul, a true child of God, by just being. When I saw a need, I plunged right in to fill it, correct it, save it, or do it right. The question "Is this my task?"

had not been examined.' In M Gilpin, *Discovering God as companion*, Author House, USA, p. 117.

31 See M Fox, *Original blessing*.

32 Eugene Stockton, *Wonder: a way to God*, St Pauls Publications, Australia, 1998.

33 Exodus Ch 16. See also, Penn: 'Wait and watch unto His daily and hourly visitations to your souls.'; 'Don't bow down thyself before thy old experiences ... Remember that the manna descended from heaven daily ... and that manna that was gathered yesterday cannot serve today for food.' Quoted in Vining ,PHP 167, p. 15.

34 See Linda Theresa, 'In the heart of pain' in M Gilpin, pp. 71-73.

35 Taber, pp. 7-8.

36 See also I Penington in Keiser & Moore 2005, pp. 151-152 from *Where is the wise? Where is the scribe?* (1660) 1.416-517.

37 I have read of someone being entranced by George Fox's bird stories. Also he regarded nature study as essential to children's education.

38 'Reverencing the Earth in the Australian Dreaming' by Miriam Rose Ungunmerr-Baumann and Frank Brennan in *Eremos*, Autumn 1990, p. 22.

39 Rex Ambler, *Light to live by*, Quaker Books, London, 2002, pp. 30-31.

40 T Canby Jones, *The Power of the Lord is over all: the pastoral letters of George Fox*, cited in Scott Martin, 'The Power: quaking and the rediscvery of primitive Quakerism', *Friends Journal*, May 2001.

41 M Fell, in Hugh Barbour, *Margaret Fell speaking*, PHP 206, 1976, p. 10. See also, R Moore, *The Light in their consciences: Early Quakers in Britain 1646-1666*, especially at p. 145 where Moore writes of *'early letters, where the "power of the Lord", unambiguously, meant quaking'*.

42 Qi Gong is energy work with movement, within the Chinese healing tradition.

43 See Fox's journal; also, Fox, *Book of miracles*, edited and with introduction and notes by Henry Cadbury, with forewords by R Jones and others, Quakers Uniting in Publications, Friends General Conference, Philadelphia, USA & Quaker Home Service, UK, 2000.

44 Marcelle Martin, *Holding one another in the Light*, PHP 382, 2006.

45 *Chakras* are psychic centres associated with the major nerve plexuses and endocrinal glands in the body. See Satyananda, *Asana pranayama mudra bandha*, pp. 331-340.

46 M Gilpin, *Discovering God as companion*, entries by Elaine Emily and Marcelle Martin.

47 M Gilpin, p. 93.

48 Michele Tarter in 'Quaking in the Light' (p. 146) wrote: 'Elders of Second Generation Quakerism ... erased any trace of "enthusiasm", or corporeal prophecy, when they rewrote

their history in the 1670's, attempting to "dignify" and save the movement in the midst of severe anti-Quaker persecutions.' See also, Richard Bailey, 'Was seventeenth century Quakerism homogeneous?' in Pink Dandelion (ed.), *The creation of Quaker theory: insider perspectives*. See also, Henry Cadbury Fox's *Book of Miracles*.

49 Tarter, 'Quaking in the Light', p. 147.

50 Tarter, p. 149.

51 In using this metaphor I do not deny the value of darkness. Anne Hosking in J Lampen (ed.) *Seeing, hearing, knowing: reflections on Experiment with Light*, William Sessions, York, England, 2008. at p. 9 wrote, 'We were conscious of the goodness of darkness, where the seed grows safely, where labour and birth so often take place, where one rests and dreams, and were grateful for the dark.'

52 In addition to Ambler's books, see J Lampen (ed.) *Seeing, hearing, knowing*.

53 As I see it, the main difference is that the Light does whatever is most needful, and sometimes this is not showing us our separation from presence, but something else – for example, Diana Lampen wrote of a time when she was unwell and very tired; during the Light Group practice she felt that she was being held like a child in her mother's arms, resting and being loved. *Seeing, hearing,knowing*, p. 30.

54 Settled meetings were established for those who were convinced (i.e. who knew and accepted Quaker practice). They are contrasted with the threshing meetings which were public meetings open to all, which could be very noisy and ecstatic..See Moore, p. 146.

55 Fox's letter to Lady Claypool, see Ambler, *Light to live by*, p. 20.

56 *To all such as complain that they want power* (1662) in I Penington, *The Works*, Vol II, Quaker Heritage Press, 1994-7, p. 297.

57 Eugene Gendlin, *Focusing*. Even better as an introduction is Anne Weiser Cornell, *The power of focusing*. Gendlin has also developed a method for creative thinking, called Thinking at the Edge.

58 Nancy Saunders, *Focusing on the Light* in J Lampen (ed.) *Seeing, hearing, knowing*, p. 37.

59 Source unknown.

60 Barclay on will-worship; quoted in Elizabeth Gray Vining, *William Penn mystic,* PHP 167.

61 William Penn, *No cross, no crown: a d iscourse showing the nature and discipline of the Holy Cross of Christ*, William Sessions Book Trust, York, England, 1981.

62 This theme runs throughout I Penington, *Knowing the mystery of life within: selected writings in their historical and theological context,* selected and introduced by R M Keiser & Rosemary Moore, especially Part II.

63   George Fox, 'To all that would know the way to the kingdom', 1653, in *Works* 4:17.

Modern English translation by Rex Ambler in *Light to live by*, pp. 8-9.

64 *Works of Margaret Fell*, pp. 95, 136, quoted in Hugh Barbour, *The Quakers in Puritan England* Yale University Press, 1964, p. 98, and in Ambler *Light to live by*, p. 5.

65 Fox: 'Don't go on looking (at the things that tempt you, confuse you, distract you and the like), but look at the light that has made you aware of them' from the Letter to Lady Claypool, in Ambler, *Light to live by*, p. 20. Brother Lawrence and Thomas Kelly also teach this.

66 Here Jesus is amplifying the great commandment in the Torah: see Leviticus 19:17-18. Jesus' older contemporary, the great Pharisaic teacher Hillel also taught a version of this; see discussion in Karen Armstrong, *The great transformation: the world in the time of Buddha, Socrates, Confucius and Jeremiah*, pp. 379-382.

67 Marshall Rosenberg, *Non violent communication: a language of life* is very good on this; see also Anne Weiser Cornell, *The power of focusing*.

68 The Hasidim are a sect of Judaism that originated in 16th century Poland as a mystical movement. Quote from *Gates of repentance*, Central Conference of American Rabbis, New York, 1984, p. 232.

69 Margaret Wilkinson herself wrote a Backhouse Lecture, *Wisdom: the inward teacher*, Australia Yearly Meeting, 1978.

3. The Meeting for Waiting Worship

The spirit deep within them would … show them the truth about themselves…
The truth would free them from their dependence on authorities and enable
them to trust their own inner resources. It would free them from fear of others
(and fear of life) and enable them to love one another and bond with one
another. Out of this a true, viable community would emerge, which would give
them all the support they needed. This would be a true 'church', the Christ
within them would be a real 'teacher and shepherd', and their own bodies
would be 'temples of God and of Christ'. That is how Fox 'turned the people
from the darkness to the light'.[1]

3.1 How individuals worship in Meeting

Centring down

Our foundational practice is just as it is for individual worship: we centre
down, become still, and empty ourselves so that we can listen to the Spirit.

The more we practise outside the Meeting, the more quickly and effectively we will centre down in Meeting, which will make it easier for the Spirit to 'gather' the worshippers. William Taber's[2] writing is very helpful on this. While he describes a number of approaches to 'entering and centering', he writes that

> most of these approaches include three important qualities. The first is *desire*, a profound yearning to be in the Presence ... the second is *focus* ... aim toward a relaxed, alert attentiveness in the presence of God. And the third is *trust, a synonym of faith*, for it takes trust to go out into the deep water; it takes trust to let go and rest or float in the deep and Living Water of the Stream.

Radiating love

I have experienced another very important practice which Taber discusses. When one has centred, emptied oneself and experienced the creative silence, then one can learn to feel the love connecting each worshipper to each other and to God, and one can radiate love[3] to each one. If the silence is to become vibrant, and the Meeting an occasion for changing lives, then it is essential that some Friends are practising in this way. These Friends' practice brings us all deeper into the Beyond Within who is at the centre of us all.

In some Meetings, several experienced Friends begin worshipping well before the scheduled time, and there is already a hushed presence in the Meeting as other Friends enter. This can make a big difference to the quality of the worship.

3.2 The gathered Meeting

Sometimes in Meeting for Worship there comes, for some, or most of us, a deepening and thickening of our silent communion. We cease to be individuals worshipping. We become united in a timeless experience of loving Presence. This communal mystical experience is awesome. We may experience profound peace, or sometimes great challenge, shaking us to our core, and transforming us. Traditionally, Quakers described such Meetings as 'gathered'. We sense a vast power flowing through us. We are knit together, deeper than words, in love.

Some worshippers can sense this flow of divine power as a physically felt shift. There are others who feel it but do not think of it in physical terms. Inner physical awareness is counter to our mainstream culture. And there are others who are not aware of the gathering of a Meeting.

While we cannot reliably create gathered Meetings, which are a gift of God, we can foster conditions which enable this gift, or, conversely, conditions that make it very unlikely. It is hugely important to foster gathered Meetings. Our lives and our relationships are transformed by such worship, usually slowly and gently, occasionally fiercely. (And, as Thomas Kelly and William Taber both say, worship is also valuable even when the Meeting does not become gathered.[4])

The Jesuit scholar Michael Sheeran[5], in his study of Quaker decision-making in Philadelphia, formed the opinion that there is a critical distinction among Friends in the liberal unprogrammed tradition. It is between those who experience the gathered Meeting, and those who do not.

Sheeran says that this is more significant than the distinction between Universalist Friends (those who favour religious pluralism) and Christo-centric Friends.[6] I think that this distinction may actually dissolve into a distinction between those whose faith and temperament are inclusive, and those who tend to exclusivism. However, one can be an *inclusive* Christian[7]; indeed, Jesus[8] himself, and many early Friends, tended to Universalism. Finding the best in the tradition one grew up with is usually a wise course, knowing that when one feels at home somewhere, then one can discover that one is at home in many places.

Currently there is a movement among us, particularly in the UK, that affirms non-theism. However, again Sheeran's distinction is more significant than the distinction between Friends who are theist, non-theist, atheist or something else. What matters is whether one can experience, or is open to learning how to experience, the gathering of a Meeting.

Whether the Meeting for Worship gathers largely depends on whether a sufficient proportion of the worshippers have faithfully practised attending to the divine energy in between Meetings. I have attended many local meetings and worshipping groups in Australia and I have rarely experienced a gathered meeting. (Of course, this could be because I am sometimes insufficiently inwardly tuned to the Divine to experience gathering). A Meeting may have Friends of longstanding, but not enough Friends who regularly practise the presence of God. One's experience of worship in such Meetings for Worship may be thin soup for nourishing the soul.

However, I have experienced the gathering of Meetings for Worship in Yearly Meeting and special learning occasions such as Meeting for Learning and retreats. On such occasions there is a greater proportion of contemplative Friends, we are separated from the world and our daily concerns for long enough to make it easier for the Spirit to gather our Meetings for Worship[9], and we worship together daily.

Everyone who attends our Meetings is infinitely precious. And if there are too many learners in proportion to those who are actually practising the presence, the practitioners can be 'swamped' and the Meeting may never settle into stillness, especially since Meetings are so short today. One balm for this problem may be to have extended Meetings for Worship.[10]

We are a far cry from the power-filled first Friends. Michele Tarter[11] has described the earliest settled Meetings for Worship:

> Together, without any leading minister, Friends would wait in sacred silence to feel divine 'currents' of God stirring in them, just as it had happened to the Apostles before them. As Fox cited with scriptural promise: 'And it shall come to pass afterward, that I will pour out my Spirit on all flesh; your sons and your daughters shall prophesy ...'(Joel 2:28-29). (Fox) declared that when spirit poured onto flesh, Friends ... experienced a concrete, substantial and visceral convincement; indeed, they 'magnified' the 'indwelling Christ' and embodied perfection on earth ... celebrating the fusion of flesh and spirit for all humankind ...Friends perceived themselves as the living texts of Christianity ... Fox told his followers that the saviour was with them, inhabiting every particle of their bodies.[12]

Early Friends developed a very practical theology: a person embodies perfection when they are living up to the 'measure' of Light that they are bodily experiencing.[13] However, as Marcus Borg has pointed out[14], we do not always interpret our mystical experiences in a way that is for the good of the individual or the community. Early Friends confronted this problem several times and gradually developed the practice of subjecting the discernment of the individual to the guidance of the Meeting as a whole. I believe that this is the way to power-filled lives such as early Friends lived.

3.3 Helps and hindrances

I offer the following statements knowing that I have myself done all the things that I now say are harmful to the Meeting – and perhaps that is why I can recognise them!

My own development as a Quaker has been very slow. I had been very deeply hurt during my childhood and adolescence. For years I could only focus on myself and on my own healing. Friends were so patient with me, and I am profoundly grateful for that. Yet gradually I did heal. The slow, gentle, persistent work of the Divine in my spirit during Meeting for Worship had much to do with that. Personal issues that had once profoundly affected me dissolved and I found myself drawn into work among Friends, organising Friends Gatherings and Light Groups. It is not for me to know now where the gentle nudges of Spirit will lead me in the future.

All the helps and hindrances affecting the individual can, of course, affect us in Meetings for Waiting Worship. We may be blocked from experiencing the gathering of the Meeting – 'angry, depressed, tired or spiritually cold … preoccupied and distracted'.[15] It is very important to attend Meeting for Worship no matter how we are feeling, and a healthy Meeting can support quite a few people feeling this way. But if it is habitual with you, then you may need help, perhaps from an elder or a therapist; certainly I found such help invaluable. In some American Meetings it is expected that each member will have recourse to a 'spiritual director': someone, not necessarily a Quaker, who is skilled at listening another person's spirit into fuller life.

3.3.1 Our offerings: Are we willing to trust and to be transformed?

Each worshipping individual, whether or not they speak, is actually bringing an offering to the Meeting for Worship, which affects the Meeting as a whole. We bring our emotions, our attitudes, our thoughts, our imaginations, and so on. We also bring our intentions and our prayers: 'May I find ease from the hurt I feel'; 'May my worship help to ease the pain between me and my brother'; and so on.

We come as we are, and all our feelings are welcome. In worship we simply offer who we are at that moment, to the Divine, in a willingness to receive the inner teaching and be transformed. It may not happen today, or next Sunday, or next month, but with a willing attitude and regular practice of worship, eventually one becomes aware of a change. However, if we are determined to hold on to negativities, as if they are who we are, then we will be blocked from learning the Quaker method of worship, with its giving over of everything to God. This harms not only ourselves, but also hinders the flow of life within the Meeting.

If we have already decided that there is nothing of value beyond that which we can put into words, then we will not experience the deeps from which new words of life come. We are likely to stay in our heads, rehearsing the past, imagining the future, or wrestling with intellectual problems.[16]

Like Deborah Shaw[17], I have found that 'the accepted Quaker canon of spiritual experience … was an intellectual one, with heart and passion to be sure, but not an embodied one.' But we cannot 'hold someone in the Light' simply through our intellects, nor can just thinking about love and humility, without a body shift, make us more loving and humble. Scepticism about, or even hostility to, our mystical bodily processes of worship will impede the flow of Spirit; not just for us, but for those worshipping with us – no, not 'with' us, for in truth we are not worshipping[18]. And if you, reading this, feel a pang that this is how you are and you want to change, then offer your doubt and your pain to the Divine, and ask trusted and experienced Friends to help you to listen within.

Sadly, a few of us come to Friends with our own agendas. We do not truly want to worship; we want to use Friends in some way. Now it is natural enough for me to come to Quakers in this condition, but it is essential that I sincerely want to open to the Spirit. If not, then this will harm the Meeting, and over time it can kill a worshipping community.

Some of us come to Quakers already regularly practising listening to and obeying the divine energy. We come in the hope of practising contemplation in community. We already have a rich inward life and practice, and we will quickly learn how to worship. The danger is that if Meetings are not deep enough, we may become disillusioned and leave.

Some come to Friends because we are passionate about acting in the world. We may be very busy. We see in Friends values that we share, and people with whom we can be friends. We may value discussion and action. We may hope to enthuse Meetings to adopt our issues and to provide us with practical support. We may have a shallow understanding of Meeting for Worship, and if we are unaware that there are deeper levels we may not be open to growth.

Inevitably, we all bring to Friends our own worldviews, the frameworks which we use to make sense of our experiences. These are always partly unconscious and they do not necessarily mesh well with Quaker practices. We need to be humble learners in the school of Christ.[19] We have a rich, nuanced tradition and the path leads all the way to holy obedience and even the few who reach that stage (and I know that I am not yet of their number) will still be humble learners all their lives.

Our most essential practice is waiting worship: emptying ourselves in stillness and silence in order to sense the presence of the Spirit. Those of us who are already inward will often find, after worshipping with Friends for some time, that we are called to action. Those who are already active may find ourselves longing for more space for transformation, often over a long period, and later we may be called to action in a different and more effective way.

3.3.2 Vocal offerings and vocal ministry

We all bring our offerings of ourselves to Meeting for Worship. Anything that someone says in Meeting is a vocal offering. Some of these are 'in the

Life'; that is, they arise from and nurture the inward experience of Presence, and only these constitute vocal ministry.[20] By their fruits you shall know whether vocal offerings are also ministry. I have included a chart setting out guidelines for determining if vocal offerings are vocal ministry. (see p. 49)

In the old days when Meetings recorded certain people as ministers, the Meetings were recognising that these people had authority to teach. However, these ministers did not speak in Meeting for Worship without an immediate 'inward motion'[21] to do so. And from the beginnings, the emphasis in vocal ministry was not on what to think, but on how to practise worship so as to experience the Life.[22] As Isaac Penington wrote, 'the end (goal) of words is to bring men to the knowledge of things beyond what words can utter'.[23] Since we discontinued the practice of recording ministers, teaching our practices in Meeting for Worship has become very unusual. This is partly because few people feel they have the authority to do so, and partly because ministry that exceeds a few sentences in length is often disapproved of. In the absence of teaching ministry, it is imperative that education is provided to those who give vocal offerings, so that they take them to heart, in worship.

We are in a quandary. We languish for lack of teaching that will help us to worship. Quakerism is not about belief but about attitudes. We become Quakers by 'convincement', becoming humble, willing to become and do what God wills. Yet often the vocal offerings in our Meetings are about belief. People think, understandably because this is what the see modelled, that they are called to give vocal ministry when they are thinking about a matter a lot, particularly if they feel strongly. However, early Quakers rejected mere 'profession' – saying the 'right' things – without 'possession' – living the life. We are in love with the words of the Peace Testimony, but are we willing to let our lives be transformed so that we speak peace? How will we live peace when the gathering storms break upon us?

Vocal offerings that are ministry will deepen the gathering or knitting together of the Meeting in love. The gathering of a Meeting takes us deeper into unity with each other in God, in widening circles. First we sense our oneness with other worshippers, then with those who are more distant from us in some way, in ever-increasing circles of love and concern until we encompass the whole of what is.

However, vocal offerings that interfere with worshippers centring down, or remaining centred, will tend to unravel the Meeting. Vocal offerings sometimes increase our agitation thereby bringing us up into the shallows. Any vocal offering arising from a negative attitude will have this effect. Such offerings take us out of the love and unity.

Some of us make vocal offerings because we are full of anxiety about the state of the world. When I am caught up in anxiety I am moving away from the Divine; if I make a vocal offering out of my anxiety, I will also increase others' anxiety and agitation. But if, despite my anxiety, I can be still and wait in the Light, it will show me my anxiety, and just in observing, there is a little distance between me and the anxiety. Seeing my anxiety in the Light does bring me closer to the Divine. If I then wait, still and silent and open, I will receive insight, truth as to what the anxiety is about and what I need to do to release it. Often there is pain in this realisation, and mourning. As I accept the truth, I am freed from fear and able to love others more, and the bonds of community are strengthened. Jesus taught letting go of fear.[24]

Preaching rushes in to fill the vacuum left when teaching withers. Here I am using the word *preaching* in the negative sense, of giving vocal offerings that tell others what the preacher thinks they should hear about and agree to.

One particularly common form of preaching is 'political' offerings or media commentary. Political offerings give people who are uncomfortable with Waiting Worship something to think about so that they do not actually have to pay attention, in stillness and silence, to the Divine. Thus political offerings entirely lack the capacity to transform anyone. Instead of tending to gather the Meeting, they tend to unravel it. People become agitated, one political offering stimulates another, and the Meeting can degenerate into a 'popcorn' Meeting in which scarcely has a speaker sat down and drawn breath than someone else is on their feet expressing upset about the human rights issue most recently in the news.

Political offerings are doubly inappropriate because they make unwelcome those who differ from most of us in political values, who might nonetheless be sincere seekers. No matter how strongly I agree with the opinions expressed, I do not accept political offerings because I want Meeting to be a safe place for all sincere seekers, regardless of politics, ethnicity, religion and sexuality.

Undoubtedly there are personal stories behind someone's strong urge to give a political offering. If only we who tend to give political ministry could reach deep within, accept our pain and find the Life beneath it. When I know something of the feelings and the needs beneath your pain or anger, I can often find unity with you. Felt deeply enough, this could become material for the Spirit to create ministry.

People's vocal offerings are often worship-sharing. Worship-sharing is a structured way of expressing what is nearest to one's heart at the moment.[25] Friends clearly desire opportunities to vent strongly held opinions, or simply to be heard, and perhaps that need can be met by worship-sharing at the close of Meeting. At Pendle Hill Meetings for Worship conclude with several minutes during which people are invited to offer silent and vocal prayers. Other meetings sometimes conclude with 'afterthoughts', offerings which did not ripen into vocal ministry.

Another kind of vocal offering which is not ministry is revelation of personal issues. These may be cries for help, and we may need in our pastoral care committees to consider what help we can provide. However, personal revelations will also agitate the worshippers. It is inevitable that worship will bring unresolved issues up and this may involve pain and grief. I think that quiet weeping in Meeting is entirely appropriate. However, if insights come and words are given, it is necessary to discern whether the words are 'bread for the community', or 'bread for home'.[26]

Finally I want to touch on a type of vocal offering which is not ministry and which is insidious because on its face it may look like the real thing. I refer to vocal offerings whose tenor is very acceptable to Friends, perhaps using words of Scripture or of early Friends, but which do not arise in the speaker at that time from the promptings of the Spirit to give vocal ministry. It is something the speaker already knows in their head, it is not felt freshly on their pulses. This is what Margaret Fell meant when she cried in her spirit, weeping, 'We are all thieves ... we have taken the Scriptures in words and know nothing of them in ourselves'.[27]

Any offering, however beautiful, which is 'out of the life', may actually quench the springs of life in other worshippers. When a worshipper has centred down and emptied their mind, they sometimes receive a stream of images or thoughts, which can be transforming. If someone then gives a vocal offering which does not arise from an inward motion, this will interrupt that stream. If someone is quaking, it will also interrupt that.[28] Sadly, many of us are so unfamiliar with bodily manifestations of Spirit that we may criticise the person involved. One very weighty Friend once told me that she 'hoped I would feel better soon' and Shaw recounts several instances of negative responses, including one where someone was actually asked to either stop quaking or leave the meeting!ature[29]

Ultimately we reach the point in worship where we will be challenged to let go of all our thoughts and imaginations, however worthy.[30] We practise stillness and silence in order to learn how to surrender our egos ('wills') to the Divine that can flow through us if we trust and let go. This surrender makes possible the group mystical experience of the gathered Meeting in which we find unity. Having let go, we are able to listen. It's not that we no longer use reason and imagination. Rather, the centre from which our reasoning and imagination arise and return is no longer the ego, but the God-in-us. In God, our reason and imagination come with a new power and truth.

How best do we receive vocal offerings? With closed eyes, relaxed and alert, I pay attention inward, and observe my response in my heart and centre. When words 'speak to my condition', they reverberate within me, and I have a physically felt shift in response. I am changed, however slightly. If I feel no response or my response is negative, I practise to let the words go and remain in, or return to, the stillness.[31] I have sometimes found this extremely difficult, as the journal entry below will elucidate. I am just learning to radiate love to the speaker, and to practise connecting with them at a level deeper

Speaking in Waiting Worship

1. Centre down

Be still

Trust

Breathe

Notice

Welcome

Thank

Empty

2. Insight arises, with a felt shift in your body.

3. Inward motion (felt shift) to speak: maybe – quake; breath and heartbeat change.

4. Is message from the Spirit or from you? God's will? No – return to 1. Yes – go to 5.

5. Is this message for you alone? Yes – go to 1. No – go to 6.

6. Is this message for the Meeting? No – go to 1. Yes – go to 7.

7. Are others likely to mistake this message for a political statement, 'sermonette,' media comment, personal revelation or announcement? Yes – go to 1. No – go to 8.

8. Do you have an inward motion to share this message right now? No – go to 1. Yes – go to 9.

9. Must you speak? Are you breathing in true love, and obedience to the Divine? No – go to 1. Yes – go to 10.

10. Yield. Stand and wait for the words to be given. Speak all and only what you have been given to share. Go to 1.

11. After Meeting, share with your elders. How did you meet the Spirit's leading? Where did you miss it? What is your sense of the effect of your speaking, on the Meeting? Do you feel that the Meeting became more, or less, gathered?

With thanks to Marcelle Martin and Chester Hill Meeting, Philadelphia, PA, and to *Quaker Life*, July/August 1997.

than words so that there can be unity between us whether the words speak to my condition or not.

Notes from my journal (1)

I became very frustrated at attending Meetings for Worship which seemed to lack life, and in which there were usually vocal offerings but little of it was ministry. I reached a crisis point … I recognised that there was a real possibility that I would do something quite inappropriate in Meeting if someone ministered in a way that pushed my buttons – maybe scream or keen or weep or run out of the room and leave Quakers forever…

Advices and Queries 12 says, in part:

> Receive the vocal ministry of others in a tender and creative spirit. Reach for the meaning deep within it, recognising that even if it is not God's word for you, it may be so for others.[32]

Some of us are sometimes very critical. We may come to Meeting so full of our own thoughts or emotions that we are unable to centre down and be truly open to vocal offerings. In this state we may 'evaluate' a vocal offering by non-Quaker standards; perhaps by how polished it is, how coherent, how well-expressed the thoughts are, how effective the delivery, how topical the subject. We may appreciate short, well-crafted discourses on sacred texts or Quaker themes. In addition, we may evaluate vocal offerings by the sincerity and conviction in someone's tone of voice.

As the Advice makes clear, vocal ministry is a word of God to us. Or sometimes vocal ministry is a word from us to God: a prayer. The test of whether a vocal offering is truly vocal ministry is whether it comes from the life in someone, the 'power of the Lord', the transforming Energy moving within them. If it does, then it will stir the Life in another or many others in the Meeting. Such ministry may be unpolished, incoherent, not well crafted, not delivered effectively, yet those worshippers who, through practice, have developed the capacity to receive Life, will be stirred and changed by it. This may be so, even if they have not heard or understood the words. As the Leni Lenape (Delaware) Indian, Papunehang, said to an interpreter about John Woolman's vocal ministry, 'I love to hear where words come from.' The tone of voice carries power.[33]

Vocal ministry proceeds from presence in the speaker to evoke or respond to presence in the listeners. Vocal ministry does not bring people out of the depths into the shallows. It helps us become more loving rather than more fearful. It moves us to experience the life and power that takes away the occasion of all wars.[34] It encourages us, makes us stronger, clearer, more adventurous.

When I have centred down and emptied myself, how do I know whether I am to give vocal ministry? On occasions when I have given vocal ministry I have found the following. Emptiness is essential. How can I listen to God if I am preoccupied with my own thoughts and imaginings? Before I enter Meeting, or during the Meeting itself, I can sense in my body that vocal ministry may come through me – feeling it within like something formless swelling into a shape about to emerge from the ocean. I experience my body gently gyrating or even being shaken; I become aware of the beating of my heart. My breathing becomes more rapid. Always, I experience energy flowing within me. I know from speaking to others who have given vocal ministry that their experiences are similar.[35] Sometimes I can feel vocal ministry swelling within me but the Meeting does not sink deep enough in the hour of worship for the ministry to ripen into speech.

Also, like Deborah Shaw[36], I have experienced quaking in meeting when I was not called to give vocal ministry.

I find it helpful, after speaking in Meeting, to talk it over with my elders. Or rather, they listen me into understanding how I have, or have not, been faithful to what was given through me. And, like John Woolman, I know what it is to weep because of my unfaithfulness. It is helpful for us to listen to each other about how the Meeting was for us, and about the currents that we discerned in the course of the Meeting.

Notes from my journal (2)

… I phoned two dear Friends who elder me to talk about my feelings of grief and frustration about vocal offerings, and this was very helpful. One of them assured me that she would be at Meeting on Sunday and would go out of Meeting with me if I left!

So I spent an hour in private worship on Sunday morning and I fasted. I did give vocal ministry and it was an extraordinary experience. I started to shake and I felt strongly called to stand up and speak but I didn't know what I was to say. As I was about to stand, someone else stood and gave a political offering. The shaking immediately ceased. After a while, the shaking, and the feeling of being called, returned … I stood up, and waited. I thought, I'll start talking gibberish. I felt real fear, stripped bare, but I had made a commitment to faithfully wait on God. Then I received a few words, which I spoke, then a few more. (I won't repeat what I said. Ministry that is 'in the Life' is unique to the particular Meeting.) *When the words stopped coming I waited for a while in case any more would be given to me, then after a time I felt clear to sit down.*

It really was extraordinary. I felt spoken through. All the things I had been thinking about ministry fell away and the words came from somewhere deeper inside. It was one time (so far, the only time) when none of the words were 'mine' and where also I spoke all the words given to me.

Later, I realised that my friend's loving presence had been very, very important. I asked her if she had been praying for me in Meeting, and she said, 'Of course'. After the Meeting we hugged each other, half-laughing and half-crying (at least I was).

And I experienced the gathering of the Meeting.

From this experience I learned a truth of which Taber speaks:

the inconspicuous, invisible ministry of people who may never speak in meeting … helps the meeting reach that state of consciousness in which minds and hearts and wills are opened and united so that the work of God may go on among us. The faithfulness of such invisible, secret ministry not only feeds and inspires gifted vocal ministry, but it also helps prepare the meeting to be receptive to life-changing ministry when it comes ... I came to realise how important are these silent, inconspicuous people who are practiced, skilled ... at just being totally present before God while engaging in the wordless prayer of lovingly holding the entire meeting up into that Presence.

Many Friends have expressed a concern that if we limit vocal offerings to vocal ministry, very little will be said in Meeting and Meetings might wither as a result. It may be helpful to worship together at length, specifically to discern the Spirit's guidance concerning the spiritual life of our Meetings for Worship.

3.4 The Experiment with Light and Meetings for Worship

Light groups resemble and differ from Meetings for Worship in some significant ways. Light groups have been designed, and are evolving, in a conscious fashion. The practice for the individual is basically the same[37], whether we are worshipping as individuals, in a Light group, or in Meeting for Worship. However, in Light groups, unlike our Meetings for Worship, we are likely to receive instruction in skills such as centring down, becoming still, opening our hearts to truth and so forth, so the practice can be very beneficial for discerning one's next step. This is a major reason why they are so transforming for many experimenters.

In Meetings for Worship, usually a few deep souls (our elders) will 'hold' the Meeting in love, as Taber describes, and this fosters the gathering of the Meeting. Similarly, when I facilitate Light groups, I hold the group 'in the Light', radiating loving energy while also remaining mindful of the world outside. Since Light group experimenters are concentrating on their own issues it might seem that there is no occasion for a gathering of the group. However, John Daly and others have noted:

how often, when we have shared our experiences that they turned out to reflect, echo or amplify those of the other people in the group. It was almost as though there was somehow a shared component in our apparently separate meditations.[38]

With an ongoing closed Light group it would be worth occasionally experimenting with a guided practice on the group itself.

There are no vocal offerings or vocal ministry in Light groups. After the guided practice, experimenters are often given an opportunity to reflect on whatever they have learned, through a quiet activity such as journalling, drawing, walking or sitting. This is followed by an opportunity for people to worship-share within the group. We often concluded Light groups held at Devonshire Street Meeting by crossing the road for coffee and refreshments, and some of our most profound insights have come at that time.

Endnotes

1 Rex Ambler's description of Fox's teaching in J Lampen (ed.), *Seeing, hearing, knowing: reflections on experiment with Light, William Sessions Ltd, York, England*, p. 4.

2 W Taber, *Four doors to Meeting for Worship*, PHP 306, p. 13.

3 Buddhist teachers also do this. When a Vipassana teacher gives me *metta* (loving kindness), I actually feel a clear impersonal love radiating through me, gently healing me. Our Meetings for Worship are also opportunities for giving and receiving healing.

4 Thomas Kelly, 'The gathered Meeting' in *The eternal promise*, Harper & Row, 1966, First Friends United Press, Richmond, Indiana, 1977, p. 86;Taber, p16. See also, Tom Gates, *Worship: 'The Gathered Meeting' revisited*, Philadelphia Yearly Meeting, c. 2008.

5 M Sheeran, *Beyond majority rule: voteless decisions in the Religious Society of Friends*, Philadelphia Yearly Meeting, Religious Society of Friends, 1996.

6 See also, Patricia Loring, *Listening spirituality, Vol II: corporate spiritual practice among Friends*, Openings Press, 1999.

7 See Marcus Borg, *The heart of Christianity: rediscovering a life of faith*, Harper, San Francisco, 2003.

8 David Johnson, 'Jesus: Universalist rather than Christian', *Australian Friend*, March 2008, p. 24. Note: I am not implying that Jesus was a Christian, he was a Jew; the first

Christian was Paul. Early Friends were inclusivist, see QFP 27.13 (Isaac Penington), 27.01 (William Penn) and 27.02 (John Woolman).

9 We are co-creators with God of the Universe (an important Jewish concept); in this sense God is not omnipotent. God cannot gather us if we are not prepared.

10 Marcelle Martin, *Invitation to a deeper communion*, PHP 366, 2003.

11 ML Tarter, 'Quaking in the Light: the politics of Quaker women's corporeal prophecy in the seventeeth-century transatlantic world' in *A centre of wonders: the body in early America*, ed. JM Lindman & ML Tarter, Cornell University Press, 2001, p147. It is clear from the context that Tarter was talking about settled Meetings of convinced Quakers. Richard Bailey, in 'Was seventeenth century Quaker Christologyhomogeneous?' in Pink Dandelion (ed), *The creation of Quaker theory: insider perspectives*, Ashgate Publishing, UK,wrote, (p. 63) 'It is one thing to speak of Christ's spiritual presence in the believer and quite another to speak of a "flesh and bone" presence as Fox did.'

12 Zablon Malenge from Nairobi Yearly Meeting also compares God to 'radio waves that are ever present and are perceptible when human instruments are properly tuned to pick them up'. Full quotation in Pink Dandelion, *An introduction to Quakerism*, Cambridge University Press, 2007, p. 208

13 Dandelion, p. 38.

14 Marcus Borg, *Jesus: uncovering the life, teachings, and relevance of a religious revolutionary*, HarperCollins, 2006, p. 319: Ch 5 endnote 12.

15 Advices and Queries nos. 10 & 12, in QFP, 2nd edn, 1995-1998, at 1.02.

16 Taber writes 'In this living Presence it becomes safe for the ego to relax … the sharp boundaries of the self can become blurred and blended as we feel ourselves more and more united with fellow worshippers and with the Spirit of God … In this state of consciousness we become aware of the reality behind (a) metaphor, of being "in the mind of Christ" as we sense that our analytical mind is now a tool rather than a master, as if it has become cushioned in a vaster mind with access to wider ways of knowing.'

17 Deborah Shaw, *Being fully present to God*, Michener Lecture, Southeastern YM of the Religious Society of Friends, 2005, p. 28.

18 This is my difficulty with some, but by no means all, non-theists. The contributors to David Boulton's book *Godless for God's sake* include sceptics and also mystics. I am generally in accord with the latter.

19 E Dunstan, QFP 11.18.

20 I am indebted to Elaine Emily of Strawberry Creek Meeting, Berkeley, California, for this concept.

21 Taber, pp. 22-24.

22 In Fox's journal there is an example where Frances Howgill rose to preach but then

desisted when he saw that the people were sitting under Christ their teacher, Nickalls edn. p. 168.

23 QFP 27.27

24 John MacMurray, *To save from fear*, Wider Quaker Fellowship, Philadelphia, 1979.

25 Worship-sharing is a Quaker group practice that cultivates both interior and outward listening: as in Meeting for Worship, we are gathered to intentionally listen for the Divine; the word 'sharing' means that, unlike in times of worship, we do not need to wait for a special prompting of the Spirit to speak. The speaking is done in a disciplined fashion, out of silent worship; see P Loring *Listening spirituality Vol 1, personal spiritual practices among Friends*, Openings Press, USA, p. 168.

26 P Loring, *Listening spirituality Vol II: corporate practices*, p. 130.

27 QFP 19.02.

28 As I have personally experienced, and as Deborah Shaw recounts in an unpublished paper, *In My Body*, written for the School of the Spirit, Pennsylvania Yearly Meeting, 2003, at p. 6.

29 Deborah Shaw, p. 30.

30 '[the mind of Christ] is present to teach thee, and judge thy wandering mind, which would wander abroad, and thy high thoughts and imaginations, and makes them subject: for following thy own thoughts thou art quickly lost.' George Fox, *Works* Vol IV, Gould, Philadelphia, 1831, p. 17.

31 Taber writes (p. 22) 'Even if the message is long and tedious, or if it seems inappropriate to us, we *can* still remain in that special state of consciousness which allows us to stay focused on God while at the same time surrounding the speaker and the rest of the meeting with love and light.'

32 The Advices and Queries are used by Friends as a kind of touchstone of our practice. I quote from QFP 1.02.

33 Phillips Moulton (ed.), *The Journal and Major Essays of John Woolman*, Friends United Press, Richmond, Indiana, 1989, p 133.

See also, Janet, *Dialogue with the Other: Martin Buber and the Quaker Experience*, PHP 192, 1973, p. 22 for a powerful example. Paul Fleischman, a Vipassana teacher, writes 'The Dhamma is both content and tone of voice' in *Cultivating inner peace*, 2nd edition, Pariyatti Press, Onalaska, WA, USA, 2004.

34 From George Fox's early [1651] statement of the Peace Testimony; 'I told [the Commonwealth Commissioners] I lived in the virtue of that life and power that took away the occasion of all wars … I told them I was come into the covenant of peace which was before wars and strife were.' In QFP 24.01.

35 See Janet Schroeder, pp. 13-14.

36 Deborah Shaw, *In my body*, unpublished paper, p. 5. She also writes about quaking when she was working on committees: 'I felt very calm and joyful, feeling that the quaking was a sign from God to remind me to say what I was given and to not worry about how or if it was received.' Similarly, in Meetings for Worship for Business I have sometimes experienced a palpable current of energy flowing up my torso, indicating that I am to speak a truth which I find difficult to say, and encouraging me.

37 The only difference is that Light group instructions focus on bringing some uneasiness to the Light, whereas early Friends' practice, and ideally practice in Meeting for Worship, would be to empty oneself and simply leave it to the Light to bring to one's attention *whatever* is needful. So, if, for example, we feel calm joy throughout the practice, perhaps this is what our souls need right now; reflecting on and incorporating into oneself the deep joys of our lives is also part of the work of the Light.

38 John Daly, 'A Quaker Jewel' in Lampen, J (ed.), *Seeing, hearing, knowing*, p. 18

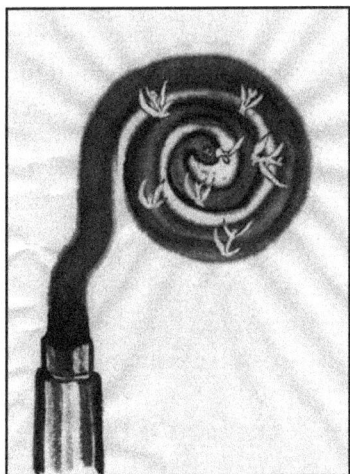

4. Quakers and the more-than-human world

Quakers are called to be peace-makers – peace within our selves, peace between self and others, peace within communities, peace between communities, and peace within the more-than-human world. We are called to be peace-makers individually and also corporately through secular corporate forms that we originated[1], and through our Meetings for Worship for Business. These Meetings use an amazing unique decision-making process[2] which merits far more space and depth than I can give it here[3], so my comments will be more general.

Whatever I think and feel, say and do affects the beings around me and vice versa. My peace-making spirals outwards from my self to all systems of which I am part, and peace-making spirals inwards, from all systems to their component beings. I sense intimations of being, and of the transformations needed in our views of and behaviour towards those beings. In very briefly calling these beings to our attention, I will spiral out from those most like ourselves, to those apparently less like ourselves. Then I will return to the wider issues of our Meeting communities and our encounter with the more-than-human world.

4.1 The spiral of being, outwards from self

Peace-making begins with the work of transformation of one's self. As I have experienced inner transformation, all my relationships have been affected. I am very thankful for skills I am learning through studying and practising Marshall Rosenberg's non-violent communication, skills creating reconciliation where I expected rupture.

I receive encouragement from dream work.[4] One night at Pendle Hill when I was doing a dream workshop, I dreamed just one vivid image: the top of a bishop's crozier[5] in the shape of a spiral with tiny new eucalyptus leaves budding out of it. Someone in the workshop told me the legend that after the death of Jesus, Joseph of Arimathea and Mary Magdalene travelled, seeking a place to stay. They would know that they had reached the right place when Joseph's staff burst into blossom. When they came to Glastonbury, the staff burst into bloom. Glastonbury is a major centre for indigenous, incarnational, nature-based British spirituality and also for Christianity. So I interpret just one meaning of the dream as follows: my native spirituality is nature-based, incarnational and Christian, and it is Australian.

And now to widen the spiral.

People

To emphasise the unity of all humans, the Buddha said, 'Everybody's tears are salty, everybody's blood is red.' Quakers have a testimony to the equality of all people. However, much of the havoc that we humans have wreaked on our home, the Earth, has been brought about through some societies dominating others.[6] In Australia, the destruction of 'country' is intricately interconnected with the destruction of the Aboriginal societies and peoples for whom that country was home and so much more (and yet they survive).[7]

Given that much of the destruction has been perpetrated by Christian and post-Christian societies, it is ironic that Jesus was a great prophet of non-violence. Jesus taught, 'Love your enemies'. But Jesus' audience were an oppressed people, whereas we Australian Quakers are almost all part of the mainstream white society which in many ways oppresses others. We are the Romans of our time, not the Jews. Just as John Woolman non-violently worked to dismantle slavery, partly by visiting one Quaker slave-owner after another, so we must begin by dismantling structures of oppression within ourselves, and challenge other Quakers to do likewise. Oppressive behaviours are tragic expressions of unmet needs. To discover the feelings, and the needs the feelings point to is difficult, painful, rewarding spiritual work.

Australia includes peoples from so many different societies. Crucial to creating a healthy Earth community is creating healthy human communities. Quakers have an opportunity to be part of the great work of melting the barriers between Australians from different ethnic backgrounds, and also between different sorts of Christians, and between people of different faiths. It is not that the differences will disappear, but that we might find a deeper unity in spirit beneath our differences. To love one another we must get to know one another. One of the most pressing tasks is for us to humbly learn from Aboriginal people. If we can accept the truth about our shared history in Australia, and mourn together, we can heal ourselves.

Animals

'Everybody's tears are salty, everybody's blood is red.' This maxim also applies to non-human animals, whether domesticated or free. They have value in themselves for themselves, and, like all beings, they are co-creators[8], through the divine energy, of the more-than-human world. We are one species among billions. When at night I hear the haunting call of the last bush stone curlew in my area, I rejoice and I weep. I rejoice for this bird's continued survival, and I weep because it belongs to a 'ghost' species, one that will become extinct in the near future, at least in New South Wales. I feel horror at the loss of the species and concern for the survival of the ecosystems of which they are part. And I think the bird is beautiful, although that is a merely human judgment.[9]

In the eye of God all birds are beautiful. To me it makes no sense to say that my life is more 'valuable' than the life of the bird. What *is* true is that my power as a co-creator with God is far greater than the bird's.

Quaker spirituality requires and creates humility: relinquishing self so that God becomes the centre of our being. And humility is now necessary for us species-wide, or we will be humiliated. May we humbly learn from this holy land and all of her beings, so that we can nourish her as she nourishes us.

Living beings

The Buddha's maxim can be viewed in a more expansive way, so as to include other living beings. Trees, plants and other life-forms are like us: they breathe, and drink; they eat and excrete, they are born, re-create their kind and die. Like us, they are subject to the rhythms of day and night, the pull of the moon's tides, magnetism and gravity. As more and more of my unconscious ripens into consciousness, I have come to know, sensuously[10], that community includes all beings.

Big Bill Neidjie of the Gagadju people who live to the west of the Alligator River in Arnhem Land, strongly emphasised human kinship with plants and trees:

> This ground never move. I'll be buried here. I'll be with my brother, my mother. If I lose this, where I'll be buried? I'm hanging onto this ground. I'll become earth again. I belong to this earth. And earth should stay with us. Tree the same as me. When he get old he'll die. He'll be dead and burn. He'll leave his ashes behind. Tree become earth.[11]

I am writing this at Pendle Hill, looking out my window at sky and clouds, American beech and linden trees, grass, red cardinal and other birds, grey squirrels, and at night the fireflies. I am reflecting that there is no 'I' apart from all of this. I am becoming dis-illusioned about our supposed individuality. We inhale the life-giving oxygen that trees exhale, and their presence nurtures us spiritually and helps to regulate temperature, atmosphere and water cycles. I choose to think that when the divine energy said, 'Let *us* (plural, feminine) make human' (Genesis 1:26), trees were among the *us*.

In Genesis 2:6 the garden is watered by a stream arising from beneath the ground, and there are many trees. Once, after rain, I put my ear to the skin of a small spotted gum, and heard the tree drink, the water hiccuping as it traversed the cell walls of the xylem, and I realised that hitherto I had actually thought of trees as non-living. We ignore their needs at our own peril. A friend in the emergency services told me of mature trees falling even on still days, and their roots were completely dry. We seem to have forgotten that trees need to drink; our actions are causing water tables to fall precipitously and trees to die of thirst.[12] Are we un-creating the Garden of Eden?

Other beings

Then there are the beings we don't think of as living. The more-than-human world can be analysed in terms of systems and their components; these include rocks, watercourses, air, and more. However, the Earth as a whole is self-regulating and so can be viewed as a living being, Gaia.[13]

Further, there are beings that we have created. If I see shoes or a bike or a car as a *being* then I am more likely to honour all that went into its making, and its eventual change into *something else*, which also has value. I will feel upset when these processes hurt other beings and I will want to work to minimise this. Recognising that one being's waste is another being's food, I will seek out 'cradle to cradle' products.[14]

Beings also include humanly created forms to which humans have given a 'body', such as Yearly Meetings and corporations. Walter Wink has symbolised the ethos or 'spirit' breathing through a particular corporate form, as a 'power' or 'angel'.[15] Some of these angels are fallen. An example is the limited liability corporation which makes profits for shareholders and huge incomes for directors, regardless of the suffering caused to other beings. Redeeming corporations and other fallen institutions is a supremely important task facing humankind.

4.2 Quakers and a great threat to peace: Earth fever

Experimental method is at the heart of modern science; it is also at the heart of Quaker religious practice. In fact, the two methods arose from the same ferment in seventeenth-century European societies. There is a very strong consensus among scientists, including Quakers, that most life on earth is threatened by global warming. I trust them. However, I find more useful a less bland term: Earth fever.

I sense a reluctance among Australian Quakers to take this issue seriously or to see it as the kind of issue with which we, as Quakers, should engage. I wonder if this partly stems from anxiety? People tend to avoid looking at death; we prefer to live in the illusion that we control our lives. Only the kind of whole-body 'knowing' that the Light reveals as we yield to God's will can remove anxiety. I am only responsible for the tasks that I am given; for the rest, I trust. Jesus told us not to be anxious about tomorrow. Now, as then, our basic choice is between fear and love.

People, and the corporate beings we have created, have unconsciously caused Earth fever by acting in ways that are not in presence. The problem is, above all, a spiritual one which requires spiritual healing. Often technical solutions are available for ecological problems, but our governance systems (which ultimately arise from our spiritualities) are unable to consistently and effectively make the necessary decisions.[16] Our legal system and government is adversarial and this fosters blame and suspicion. We must create new corporate forms based on love, creativity and community. We urgently need decision-making processes that foster truth, transparency and inclusion of the points of view of all affected parties including the non-human ones. Gerard Endenburg's sociocracy[17], derived from Quaker decision-making, is promising.

Participating in Meeting for Worship gradually transforms us as individuals, and also forms us into community. When we experience 'gathering', we are tuning in to deeper levels of awareness than conscious thought, and we are connecting with God in each other. My hope is that we may also re-learn such connections with other beings. We need ways of communicating that are deeply loving and respectful of beings. Let us practise deep, compassionate non-violent listening to those we do not know well, from other societies and from other life forms. The best time to work to create the conditions for peace is *before* violence occurs.

Whether or not our species becomes extinct, part of our task now is to become more loving, more listening, more peaceful, more present and whole, so that we flow with life in a conscious way, dying well ourselves and helping others, in dying, to trust that somehow 'all shall be well, and all shall be well, and all manner of things shall be well'.[19] I am not advocating a fatalist inertia; rather, passionate engagement with these issues without attachment to outcomes. God is not a human creation, and beyond the death of our kind, God is. I believe that God is, in some mysterious way, *dhamma*. And over eons of time, the divine energy will flow into new, non-human life forms.

4. God's time, the kingdom and the wellspring

We live in time both as *chronos*, or time according to the clock, and as *kairos*, time perceived from God-in-my-centre, flowing and ebbing according to the significance of what I am experiencing.

I'm you, and I'm OK

My father died when I was 23 months old. When I was about 3 years old I was being cared for by people who were cruel to me. My grandmother and her brother decided to take me to live with them. I had no recollection of my grandmother whatsoever. I remember travelling to be handed over to my grandmother, sitting in the back of the car, the black seats, the smell and texture of the leather. I knew that my carers could scarcely wait to get rid of me. I stared at the floor of the car, just willing it to open up and swallow me up so that the pain would stop. This was the fourth time I had been sent away.

That evening, at my grandmother's house, I went out into the back yard. The sky was deep black, and it was jewelled with stars. I raised my arms skywards, in a gesture of supplication: 'Help me. I can't take this any more.' I felt a hand reach down from the sky and touch my fingers, and a silent voice inside me said, 'I'm you and I'm grown up and I'm just fine. All is well.'

The moment of wonder faded, and, comforted, I went back inside.

Three decades later, at Yearly Meeting, sitting in Meeting for Worship, I experienced the grief and pain of that little girl and I reached down inside my heart, and touched her, and silently said, 'It's all right, I'm here and I'm OK.' It wasn't until the next year, at Yearly Meeting in Meeting for Worship, that I realised that I had experienced the kairos *moment from both ends, as a child and as an adult.*

Thus my personal mystical experience was expanded and made more meaningful in corporate worship.

What do such experiences mean for *chronos?* Can we heal our past? If so, can we redeem our future? Deborah Shaw has written about opening herself to 'the miraculous possibilities that abound for those that live in "that life and power".'[20] I have experienced this also. Such possibilities are not supernatural; they are created when one's body is very finely tuned to the more-than-human world. One Experimenter with Light, John Gray, wrote of experiencing the Light within:

> like a column going up from my lower torso and out at the top of my head. I feel reassurance, strength, groundedness, and a felt sense of connection to the wider universe.[21]

Eugene Gendlin has written:

> Your physically felt body is in fact part of a gigantic system of here and other places, now and other times, you and other people, in fact the whole universe. This sense of being bodily alive in a vast system is the body as it is felt from the inside.[22]

I believe that the Experiment with Light, and Focusing, and worshipping using our bodies as the text through which God is known to us give us skills and discernment so that miracles can happen.

Moreover, our Meetings for Worship, and Meetings for Worship for

Business, make it possible for loving divine energy to transform us and through us the world, in a way that is vastly greater than is possible through individuals.[23] Christians talk of 'the kingdom of God' which is based on the mutuality of friendship and love. Quakers often call this the 'peaceable kingdom' and as we move in our spiritual journeys through transformation into holy obedience, we increasingly inhabit and evoke this kingdom. It is both now, always and future.[24]

Once I experienced the loving divine energy that many call God as a vast underground river, springing up first in me, then in all humans, then in all living beings, then in all that is. If only we could catch the vision of our inter-connectedness, and drink deep at the wellspring, then step by step we would be given the love and the power to make on earth the peaceable kingdom.

Endnotes

1 Many charities (including the youth hostel movement, Oxfam and the Alternatives to Violence Project) were commenced, partly or entirely, by Quakers.

2 Our decision-making is based on discerning 'the sense of the Meeting'; see Barry Morley, *Beyond consensus: salvaging sense of the Meeting*, PHP 307, c. 1992.

3 I intend to publish something on Meetings for Worship for Business elsewhere.

4 See Jeremy Taylor, *Where people fly and water flows uphill: using dreams to tap the wisdom of the unconscious*, Warner Books, 1992.

5 'Crozier' also means 'cross-bearer'.

6 Rosemary Radford Ruether, 'Ecology and human liberation' in *To change the world: Christology and cultural criticism*, SCM Press Ltd, London, UK, 1981, wrote at p. 59, 'Social domination is the missing link in the question of domination of nature. The environmental crisis is basically insoluble as long as a system of social domination remains intact that allows the owners and decision-makers to maintain high profits for the few by passing on the costs to the many in the form of low wages, high prices, bad working conditions and toxic side effects of the techniques of extraction.'

7 See Susannah Brindle, *To learn a new song: a Quaker contribution towards real reconciliation with the Earth and its peoples*, James Backhouse Lecture, Australia Yearly Meeting, Religious Society of Friends (Quakers), 2000. Also, *Coming right way: 'doing justly, loving mercy and walking humbly' in Australia*, Emu Feathers Series, Yearly Meeting Indigenous Concerns Committee of the Religious Society of Friends (Quakers) in Australia, 2002.

8 For example, rabbits, cane toads, lantana and many other beings that we thoughtlessly brought here are transforming Australian landscapes.

9 Birds see things differently – they have four cones in their eyes to our three, and so have a much richer perception of colours than humans.

10 David Abram, *The spell of the sensuous: perceptions and language in a more-than-human world*, Pantheon Books, New York, 1996,.

11 Bill Neidjie, Stephen Davis & Allan Fox, *Australia's Kakadu Man: Bill Neidjie*, Resource Managers Pty Ltd, Darwin, 1986, p. 38.

12 Some places (e.g. parts of the Murray-Darling catchment) have acid sulphate soils. Our demand for water is so drying out the soils in this catchment that oxygen is reacting with them, and when the water does flow, it reacts with the soils to create sulphuric acid, sometimes as strong as battery acid, which kills everything around.

13 James Lovelock popularised this concept in his Gaia theory. See *The revenge of Gaia*, Allen Lane, UK, 2006.

14 William McDonough & Michael Braungart, *Cradle to cradle: remaking the way we make things*, North Point Press, New York, USA, (2007) 2002; see article by Matt Tyrnauer, *Vanity Fair*, May 2008, p. 102ff.

15 Walter Wink, *The powers that be: theology for a new millennium*, Galilee Books, Random House, New York, 1998.

16 See, for example, Peter Rogers, 'Facing the Freshwater Crisis' in *Scientific American*, August 2008 pp. 28-35: 'To a great extent, the technologies and policy tools required to conserve existing freshwater and secure more of it are known. What is needed now is action … Unfortunately, investment in water facilities as a percentage of gross domestic product has dropped by half in most countries since the late 1990s.'

17 John Buck & Sharon Villines, *We the people: consenting to a deeper democracy, a guide to sociocratic principles and methods*, Sociocracy Info Press, 2007. Gina Price, of West Australia Regional Meeting, is bringing sociocracy to Australia.

18 See Marielle Gilpin (ed.) *Discovering God as companion: God in Nature*, pp. 37-59.

19 Julian of Norwich, *Enfolded in love: daily readings with Julian of Norwich*, Darton, Longman & Todd, UK, 1980.

20 Deborah Shaw, 'In my body', p. 3.

21 Bronwen & John Gray, 'This we can say' in John Lampen (ed.) *Seeing, hearing, knowing: reflections on Experiment with Light*, William Sessions, York, England, 2008.

22 Source unknown.

23 See Marcelle Martin, *Invitation to a deeper communion*, PHP 366, 2003.

24 This is very similar to the progressive Jewish concept of the Messianic age. Our role in the world is one of tikkun olam, recreating the world of space-time to bring about shalom, peace.

Appendix : Australian Quakers in context

Australian Quakers are few, and scattered, although concentrated in the state and federal capital cities. As at September 2008 there are 974 adult Members, 797 adult Attenders and 232 children. There are over 50 local Meetings and worshipping groups. Australia also has one Friends school, in Hobart, which currently has an enrolment of 1300 students, very few of them Quaker. Only a very few Australian Friends have or had parents or grandparents who were Quakers. Members and Attenders under 45 may be considered young.

The word *Meeting* refers both to the event of a Meeting for Worship, and to the worshipping community attending those Meetings. The first Meeting for Worship was held in 1832. Australia Yearly Meeting was established in 1964 and since then many of us have gathered once a year for the event of one week of spiritual nurture and decision-making.

Worldwide, there are around 340,000 Quakers in three main traditions: evangelical, conservative and liberal. Dandelion[1] identifies four key theological ideas held in common:

1. the centrality of direct inward encounter with God and revelation, and thus forms of worship which allow this to be experienced: 'Quaker' was originally a nickname applied to the group because of the way they shook during worship;

2. a vote-less way of doing church business based on the idea of corporate direct guidance;

3. the spiritual equality of everyone and the idea of 'the priesthood of all believers';

4. based in part on the latter, the preference for peace and pacifism rather than war, and a commitment to other forms of social witness.

Evangelical Friends number 280 000[2] worldwide, over half of them in Kenya. They are strong in Burundi, the USA, Central and South America, and India and Far East Asia. The great majority of Friends in our Asia-West Pacific Section of Friends World Committee for Consultation (FWCC), an umbrella group, are evangelical. They call themselves Friends' Churches rather than Quaker Meetings. Their worship is facilitated by a pastor and is usually programmed, having a pre-arranged content and order, including singing. Many Friends' Churches are fundamentalist, some are modernist or follow the holiness tradition.

Conservative Friends, numbering 1500, mostly in North America, 'worship in silence, give primary authority to the direct encounter with Christ, and conserve the Quaker traditions and testimony'.

Australian Quakers are inheritors of the British liberal unprogrammed tradition, which in turn is similar in faith and practice to Yearly Meetings belonging to the United States umbrella organisation Friends General Conference (USA) and to Yearly Meetings in New Zealand, South Africa, Canada and Japan. Liberal Friends number 55 000 worldwide. With us, it is our practices that unite us, rather than our beliefs[3]. Although mostly we are liberal Christian, we include non-theists and non-Christians. In Meetings for Worship we sit in stillness and silence, centre down, and listen for the silent voice of the Inward Teacher, although individuals who feel they have a message for the Meeting may rise and speak.

Endnotes

1 Pink Dandelion, *The Quakers: A Very Short Introduction*, Oxford University Press, 2008, p. 2.

2 Figures taken from Dandelion, pp. 2, 17, 18.

3 See Robert Griswold, *Creeds and Quakers: What's belief got to do with it?*, 2005, PHP 377.

THE **JAMES BACKHOUSE** LECTURES

Backhouse Lectures, as well as other Australia Yearly Meeting publications,
are available from Friends Book Sales, PO Box 181, Glen Osmond, South
Australia 5064, Australia. Email <sales@quakers.org.au>.

www.ingramcontent.com/pod-product-compliance
Lightning Source LLC
Chambersburg PA
CBHW031330040426
42443CB00005B/280